Principles in Practice

The Principles in Practice imprint offers teachers concrete illustrations of effective classroom practices based in NCTE research briefs and policy statements. Each book discusses the research on a specific topic, links the research to an NCTE brief or policy statement, and then demonstrates how those principles come alive in practice: by showcasing actual classroom practices that demonstrate the policies in action; by talking about research in practical, teacher-friendly language; and by offering teachers possibilities for rethinking their own practices in light of the ideas presented in the books. Books within the imprint are grouped in strands, each strand focused on a significant topic of interest.

Adolescent Literacy Strand

Adolescent Literacy at Risk? The Impact of Standards (2009) Rebecca Bowers Sipe

Adolescents and Digital Literacies: Learning Alongside Our Students (2010) Sara Kajder

Adolescent Literacy and the Teaching of Reading: Lessons for Teachers of Literature (2010) Deborah Appleman

Rethinking the "Adolescent" in Adolescent Literacy (2017) Sophia Tatiana Sarigianides, Robert Petrone, and Mark A. Lewis

Restorative Justice in the English Language Arts Classroom (2019) Maisha T. Winn, Hannah Graham, and Rita Renjitham Alfred

Writing in Today's Classrooms Strand

Writing in the Dialogical Classroom: Students and Teachers Responding to the Texts of Their Lives (2011) Bob Fecho

Becoming Writers in the Elementary Classroom: Visions and Decisions (2011) Katie Van Sluys

Writing Instruction in the Culturally Relevant Classroom (2011) Maisha T. Winn and Latrise P. Johnson

Writing Can Change Everything: Middle Level Kids Writing Themselves into the World (2020) Shelbie Witte, editor

Growing Writers: Principles for High School Writers and Their Teachers (2021) Anne Elrod Whitney

Literacy Assessment Strand

Our Better Judgment: Teacher Leadership for Writing Assessment (2012) Chris W. Gallagher and Eric D. Turley

Beyond Standardized Truth: Improving Teaching and Learning through Inquiry-Based Reading Assessment (2012) Scott Filkins

Reading Assessment: Artful Teachers, Successful Students (2013) Diane Stephens, editor

Going Public with Assessment: A Community Practice Approach (2018) Kathryn Mitchell Pierce and Rosario Ordoñez-Jasis

Literacies of the Disciplines Strand

Entering the Conversations: Practicing Literacy in the Disciplines (2014) Patricia Lambert Stock, Trace Schillinger, and Andrew Stock

Real-World Literacies: Disciplinary Teaching in the High School Classroom (2014) Heather Lattimer

Doing and Making Authentic Literacies (2014) Linda Denstaedt, Laura Jane Roop, and Stephen Best

Reading in Today's Classrooms Strand

Connected Reading: Teaching Adolescent Readers in a Digital World (2015) Kristen Hawley Turner and Troy Hicks

Digital Reading: What's Essential in Grades 3–8 (2015) William L. Bass II and Franki Sibberson

Teaching Reading with YA Literature: Complex Texts, Complex Lives (2016) Jennifer Buehler

Teaching English Language Learners Strand

Beyond "Teaching to the Test": Rethinking Accountability and Assessment for English Language Learners (2017) Betsy Gilliland and Shannon Pella

Community Literacies en Confianza: *Learning from Bilingual After-School Programs* (2017) Steven Alvarez

Understanding Language: Supporting ELL Students in Responsive ELA Classrooms (2017) Melinda J. McBee Orzulak

Writing across Culture and Language: Inclusive Strategies for Working with ELL Writers in the ELA Classroom (2017) Christina Ortmeier-Hooper

Students' Rights to Read and Write Strand

Adventurous Thinking: Fostering Students' Rights to Read and Write in Secondary ELA Classrooms (2019) Mollie V. Blackburn, editor

In the Pursuit of Justice: Students' Rights to Read and Write in Elementary School (2020) Mariana Souto-Manning, editor

Already Readers and Writers: Honoring Students' Rights to Read and Write in the Middle Grade Classroom (2020) Jennifer Ochoa, editor

Children's and YA Literature Strand

Challenging Traditional Classroom Spaces with YA Literature: Students in Community as Course Co-Designers (2022) Ricki Ginsberg

Challenging Traditional Classroom Spaces with YA Literature

Students in Community as Course Co-Designers

Ricki Ginsberg
Colorado State University

NCTE National Council of Teachers of English

340 N. Neil St., Suite #104, Champaign, Illinois 61820
www.ncte.org

Staff Editor: Bonny Graham
Imprint Editor: Cathy Fleischer
Interior Design: Victoria Pohlmann
Cover Design: Pat Mayer
Cover Image: Kellee Moye

NCTE Stock Number: 05351; eStock Number: 05375
ISBN 978-0-8141-0535-1; eISBN 978-0-8141-0537-5

Library of Congress Cataloging-in-Publication Data

Names: Ginsberg, Ricki, author.
Title: Challenging traditional classroom spaces with YA literature : students in community as course co-designers / Ricki Ginsberg, Colorado State University.
Description: Champaign, Illinois : National Council of Teachers of English, [2022] | Series: Principles in practice. Children's and YA literature strand | Includes bibliographical references and index. | Summary: "Explores how high school ELA teachers, using communities of practice as a guiding framework, can work with students to build a community that defines their purposes together, harnessing the potential of YA literature and critical freedom to co-develop YA electives and lead literate lives together as a community of practice that is engaged with their local and global communities"—Provided by publisher.
Identifiers: LCCN 2022014428 (print) | LCCN 2022014429 (ebook) | ISBN 9780814105351 (trade paperback) | ISBN 9780814105375 (adobe pdf)
Subjects: LCSH: Young adult literature—Study and teaching (Secondary) | Student participation in curriculum planning. | Youth—Books and reading.
Classification: LCC PN1008.8 .G58 2022 (print) | LCC PN1008.8 (ebook) | DDC 809/.892830712—dc23/eng/20220706
LC record available at https://lccn.loc.gov/2022014428
LC ebook record available at https://lccn.loc.gov/2022014429

Dear Reader,

As a former high school teacher, I remember the frustration I felt when the gap between Research (and that is, by the way, how I always thought of it: Research with a capital *R*) and my own practice seemed too wide to ever cross. Research studies—those sterile reports written by professional and university researchers—often seemed so out of touch with the issues that most concerned me when I walked into my classroom every day. These studies were easy to ignore, in part because they were so distant from my experiences and in part because I had no one to help me see how that research could impact my everyday practice.

Although research has come a long way since then, as more and more teachers take up classroom-based inquiry, this gap between research and practice unfortunately still exists. Quite frankly, it's hard for even the most committed classroom teachers to pick up a research article or book, figure out how that research might apply to their classroom, convince their administrators that a new way of teaching is called for, and put it into practice. While most good teachers instinctively know that there is something to be gained from reading research, who realistically has the time or energy for it?

That gap informs the thinking behind this book imprint. Called Principles in Practice, the imprint publishes books that look carefully at the research-based principles and policies developed by NCTE and put those policies to the test in actual classrooms. The imprint naturally arises from one of the missions of NCTE: to develop policy for English language arts teachers. Over the years, many NCTE members have joined committees and commissions to study particular issues of concern to literacy educators. Their work has resulted in a variety of reports, research briefs, and policy statements designed both to inform teachers and to be used in lobbying efforts to create policy changes at the local, state, and national levels (reports that are available on NCTE's website, www.ncte.org).

Through this imprint, we are creating collections of books specifically designed to translate those research briefs and policy statements into classroom-based practice. The goal behind these books is to familiarize teachers with the issues behind certain concerns, lay out NCTE's policies on those issues, provide resources from research studies to support those policies, and—most of all—make those policies come alive for teacher-readers.

This book is part of the eighth series in the imprint, a series that focuses on teaching children's and young adult literature. Each book in the series highlights a different way to think about this important topic—whether you're a classroom teacher or an English educator—immersing you in the research principles surrounding the topic (as laid out in the NCTE position statement *Preparing Teachers with Knowledge of Children's and Young Adult Literature*) and then taking you into actual classrooms to see how the principles play out. Each book closes with a teacher-friendly bibliography.

Good teaching *is* connected to strong research. We hope that these books help you continue the good teaching that you're doing, think hard about ways to adapt and adjust your practice, and grow even stronger in the vital work you do with kids every day.

Best of luck,

Cathy Fleischer

Cathy Fleischer

Contents

Acknowledgments

This book wouldn't be possible without a whole community of people supporting and guiding me. My first and biggest thanks is to my partner, Rob, and three children—Henry, Ben, and Charlie. For Rob, who has supported our family with his love and always encouraged me to put my heart into everything. For my children, who reminded me that the book *must* have pictures and who provided constant hugs while I wrote.

Thank you to my relatives for the steady, continued support, and for helping me raise my children from afar—and your creativity in doing so. Mom, Dad, Cliff, Claire, Betty, Steve, Aunnie, Rena, Larry, Alan, Rikki, Sam, Nate, I love you all. Ada, Hannah, and Winston, you push me to imagine the possibilities. And to all of my relatives and elders for checking in—thank you. I am grateful for my children's teachers for checking in on me regularly and urging me forward when I sometimes entered your classrooms looking exhausted and unkempt. And to the Wulffs for your never-ending support, love, and kid-watching.

I am grateful for the bobcat who visited my back screen door more than once to keep me (very) awake and writing, for the mouse who coexisted in my late night writing room and kept me company, and for the mountain lion who scared me so much that I pulled an all-nighter. I won't be able to think of this book without remembering these three relatives.

This book started with an idea with my longtime mentor and one of my dearest friends and sister-scholars, Wendy Glenn. We placed it aside and worked on other projects, and she encouraged me to take the original idea and expand it. Her voice whispers through the entire book. Without her belief in me, I wouldn't be where I am today. I could write an entire book thanking her for all she has done for me. This woman has my heart.

It is no secret that academia can feel like an isolating place, yet colleagues and mentors have regularly lifted me up and supported me when I felt doubt. They ask no questions and love tirelessly. Within my more immediate community in the CSU English education crew this year, thank you to Kelly Burns, Cindy O'Donnell-Allen, and Louann Reid for always making me think differently and for supporting me every step of the way. Within the CSU Center for Educator Preparation, thank you to Antonette Aragón, Vincent Basile, and Kara Coffino for grounding me with your passion and commitment to teacher education and to young people. Kara, thank you especially for reading sections of this book and offering feedback. Within my CSU writing group in the years I wrote this book—Jessica Jackson and OiYan Poon—the varied coffee shops and breakfast burritos kept us going, and I wouldn't have a book without you both. At the university outside of English and education, I have felt consistently inspired by colleagues who engage with community meaningfully and with their whole selves. Roe Bubar, Dominique David-Chavez, Susan Faircloth, Jamie Folsom, Jan Iron, Tiffani Kelly, Doreen Martinez, Arlene Nededog, Danita Ordaz, Lindsey Schneider, Ty Smith, and Leslie Taylor—you inspire me regularly, and your care for place and people pushes me in ways that words can't seem to grasp. Thank you.

Outside of my university, I am grateful for Chloe Kannon for being a sister to me and always reminding me I am good enough. Every conversation we have lifts me up. For Antero Garcia for offering his friendship before he even knew me and for serving as one of my first mentors when I was a junior faculty member and unsure of my place. I've been grateful to continue to have Ashley Cartun and Dani King-Watkins as support systems (scholarly and mama-ly) as we entered a preservice teacher program, doctoral program, and then academia together. And to Kellee Moye for always inspiring me with her diligence as a faithful blog partner and shared passion for books and for young people.

ALAN colleagues, this book would not be here without the constant support of the leaders, volunteers, and friends of the Assembly on Literature for Adolescents of NCTE. There are many people who keep ALAN going and going, and these are the people who make me whole. We exchange a few thousand emails per year. It would be impossible for me to name all of the members of the ALAN organization who have inspired me and who are *doing the work* of this book in their schools and classrooms. The 2020 ALAN leadership includes: Jennifer Ansbach, Arianna Banack, Steve Bickmore, Robert Bittner, Jim Blasingame, Daria Bliss, Alyssa Chrisman, Shanetia P. Clark, Alison Daniels, Jewel Davis, Sarah J. Donovan, E. Sybil Durand, Shalonda Foster, Susan Groenke, Courtney Johnson, Nancy Johnson, Danielle King-Watkins, Mark Letcher, Vic Malo-Juvera, Suzanne Metcalfe, Caitlin Metheny, Lisa Morris-Wilkey, Jon Ostenson, Keisha Rembert, Lizette Serrano, Hunter Strickland, Julia E. Torres, and Sarah Ressler Wright. I could write pages about how each of these people has impacted me as a scholar and teacher and has worked to promote young adult literature as a force in this world. These are just some, *some* of the people of ALAN who have helped keep this organization afloat to continue to promote YA literature. Many came before and many will come after in leadership positions; this is very much a nonexhaustive list of ALAN officers. One of those people who has always believed in me is Jennifer Buehler. Her book about YA literature inspired me, and she encouraged me more than once to write my own. And Jim Blasingame—one of the greatest storytellers I know. The people of the ALAN organization have made me feel as though I have a scholar family outside of my university. ALAN friends inspire me regularly with their passionate contributions to the field and ongoing service to promote YA literature and its strength and capacity for classrooms and libraries. Thank you to the teacher contributors, many of whom are ALAN members, who willingly shared their words in the vignettes to offer authentic examples.

Quite frankly, I could write dozens of pages about the English education and literacy scholars who inspire me. Instead, I aimed to cite them in this book whenever possible to share their work with you.

I am grateful for the NCTE team for believing in this book. Kurt Austin, thank you for your regular support, and Emily Kirkpatrick, you are a fearless leader and I admire you. Bonny Graham, thank you for your beautiful way with words.

A gigantic thank you to my editor, Cathy Fleischer, who worked her magic again and again to make this book so much better than it ever could have been. She is a steady presence that every writer should have in their lives. I will be forever grateful to her for her regular encouragement and wisdom.

And last, thank you to my students—past and present—from Rockville High School, the University of Connecticut, and Colorado State University. Many have graduated, become teachers, and are now some of my closest friends. Their ideas and revisions for course design, approaches, and texts are woven through this book, and I think of them every day and am reminded how much I love my job and how fortunate I have been.

Preparing Teachers with Knowledge of Children's and Young Adult Literature

This statement, formerly known as Preparing Teachers with Knowledge of Children's and Adolescent Literature, *was updated in July 2018 with the new title,* Preparing Teachers with Knowledge of Children's and Young Adult Literature.
Originally created by NCTE Children's Literature Assembly (CLA), 2004; revised July 2018.

Overview

Purpose: Given increased calls for diversity in the English language arts curriculum and growing awareness of the need for young people to see themselves in the books they read, NCTE has commissioned an updated statement on preparing teachers with knowledge of children's and young adult literature.

Key Message: Research shows that when students are given the chance to read books that respect the questions, challenges, and emotions of childhood and adolescence, they read with greater interest and investment (Buehler, 2016; Mueller, 2001). Research also shows that teachers who are readers themselves do a better job of engaging their students in reading (Morrison, Jacobs, & Swinyard, 1999). Thus, teacher educators must support preservice teachers as they build rich and deep knowledge of children's and young adult literature over the course of their certification programs. Then teachers must invest in their own continued growth, learning, and development as children's and young adult literature advocates throughout their professional lives.

Context: A committee of English educators has updated NCTE's 2004 statement *Preparing Teachers with Knowledge of Children's and Adolescent Literature* by calling teachers at all stages of their careers to cultivate knowledge of books for young people, be readers of these books themselves, affirm diversity in book selection, and teach children's and young adult literature in ways that honor the books' literary quality as well as their potential to spark personal and social transformation.

Statement

Evidence indicates that teachers' knowledge of children's and young adult literature is inconsistent and uneven from community to community, school to school, and classroom to classroom. Preservice teachers do not read any more than the general population (McKool & Gespass, 2009). Many of today's teachers have never taken a class in children's and young adult literature, and some states have eliminated the requirement for a dedicated course in children's and/or young adult literature for teaching certification. A growing number of schools no longer employ a librarian, who may be the only professional in the building who has formal training in children's and young adult literature, collection development, and

Preparing Teachers with Knowledge of Children's and Young Adult Literature

matching young readers with books. Without librarians, the burden for reading advisory and material selection falls to classroom teachers, who often lack the training needed to perform these tasks.

Therefore, teacher education programs have the opportunity—and the responsibility—to

- *introduce* preservice teachers to books for children and teens;
- *develop* preservice teachers' understanding of the inherent value of these books for both general reading and classroom use;
- *raise* preservice teachers' awareness of the power of these books to affirm lived experience, create empathy, catalyze conversations, and respect the questions, challenges, and emotions of childhood and adolescence;
- *call* preservice teachers to embrace the roles of reading advocate and book matchmaker alongside their work as implementers of curriculum;
- *inspire* preservice teachers to commit to reading these books throughout their professional lives;
- *cultivate* in preservice teachers a commitment to teaching these books in ways that honor their literary quality as well as their potential to spark personal and social transformation;
- *build* preservice teachers' capacity for continued growth, learning, and development as advocates of children's and young adult literature.

As an organization, NCTE compels teachers at all stages of their careers to invest in books for young people—as readers of those books and as advocates for their worth in the classroom.

Recommendations

NCTE recommends that teacher educators and teachers commit to the following four principles in the service of increasing their ability to teach and advocate for children's and young adult literature.

1. Know the literature.

Preservice teachers should cultivate book knowledge throughout various methods courses and across their entire teacher preparation program, regardless of state certification requirements. They should develop broad and sustained knowledge of quality books in the fields of children's and young adult literature, including fiction, nonfiction, and multimodal texts.

At the same time, they should build knowledge of resources—including review journals, websites and blogs, social media discussions, book awards, and author appearances at local libraries and bookstores—that can provide them with information about quality new books and their potential for classroom use and reading advisory.

They should also invest in relationships with librarians and organizations such as NCTE and ALAN (Assembly on Literature for Adolescents of NCTE) that can help them build

Preparing Teachers with Knowledge of Children's and Young Adult Literature

capacity to discuss and recommend books, evaluate literature, remain current, and discover new ways to teach children's and young adult literature effectively.

2. Be readers.

Teachers who are engaged readers do a better job of engaging students as readers. According to Morrison, Jacobs, and Swinyard (1999), "perhaps the most influential teacher behavior to influence students' literacy development is personal reading, both in and out of school" (p. 81). Teachers should commit to leading literate lives and becoming connected to reading communities—whether in person or through social media—that support them as readers and literacy professionals. Teachers should understand the value of different modes and platforms for reading (Garcia & O'Donnell-Allen, 2015) and build their capacity to read with a critical, discerning eye (Newkirk, 2011).

3. Affirm diversity and exercise critical literacy.

In alignment with NCTE's Resolution on the Need for Diverse Children's and Young Adult Books (2015), NCTE challenges teachers and teacher educators to assume a transformative activist stance (Stetsenko, 2016) that supports a future of equality for all youth by engaging students with diverse books, which offer readers what scholar Rudine Sims Bishop (1990) calls windows, mirrors, and sliding glass doors. It is essential that youth have access to books in which they can see themselves and engage with the lives of others (see, for example, platforms created by the current and former National Ambassadors for Young People's Literature, including Jacqueline Woodson, Gene Luen Yang, and Walter Dean Myers). NCTE believes that books help readers transform their lives and expand their visions of the world.

Nevertheless, there is a dearth of diverse books for youth in the United States as seen in yearly statistics about trends in multicultural children's book publishing prepared by the Cooperative Children's Book Center (CCBC) of the School of Education at the University of Wisconsin–Madison. The #WeNeedDiverseBooks and #ReadInColor social media campaigns have illuminated the paucity of diverse books in the marketplace. Although the CCBC recently observed that children's picture books feature an increased number of characters with "brown skin . . . of unspecified race or ethnicity, with no visible culturally specific markers in either the story or the art," the CCBC questions whether books with racially ambiguous characters provide actual windows, mirrors, and sliding doors for today's readers (Horning, Lindgren, Schliesman, & Tyner, 2018, n.p.). NCTE joins the CCBC in urging educators to not only advocate for more authentically diverse children's and young adult books from US publishers, but also to support authors, illustrators, publishers, and booksellers whose work represents multiple perspectives and cultural diversity in the lives of all children.

In addition to being advocates and supporters of diverse literature for youth, educators who assume a transformative activist stance must build their capacities for discernment and critical evaluation so they are prepared to choose children's and YA books wisely and strategically from the books available to them. Simply because a book features diverse

Preparing Teachers with Knowledge of Children's and Young Adult Literature

characters does not mean that the book endorses equality and/or cultural understanding (Apol, Sakuma, Reynolds, & Rop, 2003; Dávila, 2012). For example, some popular works of contemporary, "multicultural" realistic fiction privilege the assumption that all residents of the United States should embrace dominant mainstream culture [e.g., *My Name is Yoon* (Recorvitis, 2003); *One Green Apple* (Bunting, 2006)]. Some of these books reinforce assimilation social narratives (Yoon, Simpson, & Haag, 2010) and/or endorse monocultural language and identity (Ghiso & Campano, 2013). Educators and students should collectively cultivate critical literacy practices to critique the social narratives that are endorsed by the books they select (Leland, Lewison, & Harste, 2012; Morrell, 2007) and talk back to the literature (Enciso, 1997).

Educators who affirm diversity and exercise critical literacy as part of a transformative activist stance recognize that they are always learning and expanding their capacities for transformation. They are open to guiding difficult discussions about inequality with students and are willing to tolerate the possibilities of "wobbling" while they explore uncharted territories with students (e.g., Fecho, 2005; Garcia & O'Donnell-Allen, 2015). They recognize that children's books are political (Nodelman, 2008; Stephens, 1992) and are the artifacts of the authors', illustrators', and/or publishers' views of the world (Willis & Harris, 2003) and/or US history (Thomas, Reese, & Horning, 2016). Moreover, these educators follow national conversations via media and blogs about diverse books, especially related to issues of power and representation (e.g., Reading While White; American Indians in Children's Books).

4. Use appropriate pedagogy.

Teaching children's and young adult literature is about more than getting students to fall in love with reading. Preservice teachers also need to learn appropriate and effective strategies for helping students find books that will engage them as readers and as participants in critical, significant conversations about their lives (NCTE, 2006; Tschida, Ryan, & Ticknor, 2014). This requires a deep knowledge of excellent books and the willingness to carefully curate a classroom library that provides appropriate choices for all students (Crisp, Knezek, Quinn, Bingham, Girardeau, & Starks, 2016; NCTE, 2017). Preservice teachers also need to know evidence-based strategies for supporting student knowledge of literary crafting—that is, how authors develop characters, construct plots, and employ other literary elements to create an exemplary work. Examining literary craft does not mean that the focus is on dissecting a book's structure or meaning. Rather, teachers should be skilled at helping students develop a common language for determining what makes a book excellent literature. Finally, teachers need to know how to advocate for the freedom and autonomy to create classrooms that support research-based pedagogical strategies for teaching children's and young adult literature (Mathis et al., 2014; NCTE Children's Literature Assembly, 2004).

Preparing Teachers with Knowledge of Children's and Young Adult Literature

Works Cited

Apol, L., Sakuma, A., Reynolds, T. M., & Rop, S. K. (2003). "When can we make paper cranes?" Examining pre-service teachers' resistance to critical readings of historical fiction. *Journal of Literacy Research, 34*,429–464.

Bishop, R. Sims (1990). Mirrors, windows, and sliding glass doors. *Perspectives, 1*(3), ix–xi.

Buehler, J. (2016). *Teaching reading with YA literature: Complex texts, complex lives*. Urbana, IL: NCTE.

Bunting, E. (2006). *One green apple*. New York, NY: Houghton Mifflin.

Crisp, T., Knezek, S. M., Quinn, M., Bingham, G., Girardeau, K., and Starks, F. (2016). "What's on our bookshelves? The diversity of children's literature in early childhood classroom libraries." *Journal of Children's Literature 42*(2), 29–42.

Dávila, D. (2012). In search of the ideal reader for children's non-fiction books about el Día de Los Muertos. *Journal of Children's Literature, 38*(1), 16–26.

Enciso, P. (1997). Negotiating the meaning of difference: Talking back to multicultural literature. In T. Rogers & A. Soter (Eds.), *Reading across cultures* (pp. 13–41). New York, NY: Teachers College Press.

Fecho, B. (2001). "Why are you doing this?" Acknowledging and transcending threat in a critical inquiry classroom. *Research in the Teaching of English, 36*(1), 9–37.

Garcia, A., & O'Donnell-Allen, C. (2015). *Pose, wobble, flow: A culturally proactive approach to literacy instruction*. New York, NY: Teachers College Press.

Ghiso, M., & Campano, G. (2013). Ideologies of language and identity in U.S. children's literature. *Bookbird, 51*(3), 47–55.

Goldstein, D. (2015). *The teacher wars: A history of America's most embattled profession*. New York, NY: Anchor.

Horning, K., Lindgren, M., Schliesman, M. & Tyner, M. (2018). A few observations: Literature in 2017. *CCBC Choices 2018*. Madison, WI: Cooperative Children's Book Center. Retrieved from: http://ccbc.education.wisc.edu/books/choiceintro18.asp

Leland, C., Lewison, M., & Harste, J. (2012). *Teaching children's literature: It's critical*. New York, NY: Routledge.

Mathis, J. B., Aziz, S., Crisp, T., Graff, J. M., Kesler, T., Liang, L. A., Sekeres, D. C., & Wilfong, L. (2014). Teaching children's literature in the 21st century. *Journal of Children's Literature, 39*(1), 56–61.

McKool, S. S., & Gespass, S. (2009). Does Johnny's reading teacher love to read? How teachers' personal reading habits affect instructional practices. *Literacy Research and Instruction,48*(3), 264–276.

Morrell, E. (2007). *Critical literacy and urban youth: Pedagogies of access, dissent, and liberation*. New York, NY: Routledge.

Morrison, T. G., Jacobs, J. S., & Swinyard, W. R. (1999). Do teachers who read personally use recommended literacy practices in their classrooms? *Literacy Research and Instruction, 38*(2), 81–100.

Preparing Teachers with Knowledge of Children's and Young Adult Literature

Mueller, P. N. (2001). *Lifers: Learning from at-risk adolescents*. Portsmouth, NH: Heinemann.

National Council of Teachers of English. (2006). *Resolution on preparing and certifying teachers with knowledge of children's and adolescent literature*. Urbana, IL: NCTE.

National Council of Teachers of English. (2015). *Resolution on the need for diverse books*. Urbana, IL: NCTE.

National Council of Teachers of English. (2017). *Statement on classroom libraries*. Urbana, IL: NCTE.

NCTE Children's Literature Assembly. (2004). *Preparing teachers with knowledge of children's and adolescent literature*. Urbana, IL: NCTE.

Newkirk, T. (2011). *The art of slow reading: Six time-honored practices for engagement*. Portsmouth, NH: Heinemann.

Nodelman, P. (2008). *The hidden adult*. Baltimore: The Johns Hopkins University Press.

Recorvitis, H. (2003). *My name is Yoon*. New York, NY: Farrar, Straus and Giroux.

Stephens, J. (1992). *Language and ideology in children's fiction*. New York, NY: Longman.

Stetsenko, A. (2016). *The transformative mind: Expanding Vygotsky's approach to development and education*. New York, NY: Cambridge University Press.

Thomas, E., Reese, D., & Horning, K. (2016). Much ado about *A fine dessert*: The cultural politics of representing slavery in children's literature. *Journal of Children's Literature, 42*(2), 6–17.

Tschida, C., Ryan, C., & Ticknor, R. (2014). Building on windows and mirrors: Encouraging the disruption of "single stories" through children's literature. *Journal of Children's Literature, 40*(1), 28–39.

Willis, A., & Harris, V. (2003). Preparing preservice teachers to teach multicultural literature. In J. Flood, S. Brice Heath, & D. Lapp (Eds.), *Handbook of research on teaching literacy through the communicative and visual arts* (pp. 460–469). New York, NY: Macmillan Library Reference USA.

Yoon, B., Simpson, A., & Haag, C. (2010). Assimilation ideology: Critically examining underlying messages in multicultural literature. *Journal of Adolescent & Adult Literacy, 54*(2), 109–118.

Statement Authors

This document was revised by an NCTE working committee comprising the following:

Jennifer Buehler, Chair – Saint Louis University, St. Louis, MO

Denise Dávila – The University of Texas at Austin

Amy McClure – Ohio Wesleyan University, Delaware, OH

Donalyn Miller – Author and Consultant, Colleyville, TX

Chapter One

Inviting Students to Design Spaces for Themselves and Their Communities with YA Literature

What is the first unit you taught for each of your classes this year? How did that unit fit into the design for the overall course? When we design courses, we typically think about units based on a whole-class focal text (e.g., *Romeo and Juliet*), overarching theme (e.g., What does it mean to be an American?), or standards (e.g., fulfilling a Common Core State Standard about writing arguments with supportive claims). In this book, I seek to disrupt the traditional ways in which we design courses to foster more ethical, community-based approaches to curricular design and instruction, to allow students to become the designers of their course experiences in ways that are meaningful to their lives and their communities.

Our classrooms are not authentically student-centered spaces when we, the teachers, design unit plans before we meet our students. Students are not centered in instruction if they walk into a school or a classroom that is already built for them. This text offers approaches that position our students as the architects of their own learning, as we learn alongside them. Not doing so results in impoverished discourse that isn't considering student voice and isn't situated within local communities and the global context. I have intentionally included the voices of middle and high school teachers who work in our teacher and librarian communities and are doing this work of centering students as architects of their learning, engaging students as partners in their communities. Their course design choices position students as critically conscious agents and motivated citizens who are invited to sit at the decision-making table of their own education and encouraged to think about how this table can invite others from their community in conversation.

Rethinking Text-Based Practices

I focus on young adult literature specifically in this text because of its dynamic, contemporary applications and its ability to offer classroom communities powerful, relevant opportunities to engage in a co-constructed course design process that centers students' lives and real-world issues. Canonical texts (along with often accompanying traditional pedagogical approaches) simply aren't working in schools. For a variety of historical, societal, and systemic reasons, certain titles are valued highly in the culture of most US schools—to the point that they drive course design and instruction. In a typical classroom, a yearlong plan for American Literature begins with the texts first: *The Crucible* or *To Kill a Mockingbird* or *The Great Gatsby* or *The Catcher in the Rye* or [insert canonical text here]. Or ninth grade revolves around reading *Romeo and Juliet* or *The Odyssey* or [insert canonical title here]. Occasionally, in the name of relevance, a more contemporary title makes its way into the mix, yet the texts consistently seem to drive the learning, and units are often designed around a central text.

We know that schools were built to teach and promulgate white, Protestant beliefs (Goldstein, 2015), and critical scholars and theorists have long claimed there is a hidden curriculum that serves to reproduce inequities in schools and society (see, for instance, Apple, 1971, 1980). It's been over forty years since some of these texts exposing the hidden curriculum were published, yet the canonical texts we use in classrooms are the same books (sometimes literally the exact same books) as those used in our (grand)parents' classrooms.

It doesn't have to be this way. Classrooms should be just as dynamic as the world around us. We have to acknowledge that we exist in spaces that were not designed to support all students, but that doesn't mean we can't work with students to intentionally interrupt and disrupt hegemonic structures.

Classic texts are not typically relevant or engaging for our students, which is not surprising since they were never intended to be read and appreciated by teens. In other words, we are teaching texts that weren't written for our students. Conversations with students repeatedly reveal that, even when these titles are assigned, they are not regularly read. In fact, a good portion of our students (one in three twelfth graders in one study) report that they don't read at all (Twenge et al., 2019). (Most of those surveyed are likely thinking about reading in reference to book-length texts, which is a more traditional conception of reading . . . but that's a topic for another book.) Although many variables likely contribute to the fact that a sizeable number of students don't read, we have to recognize that some of the major contributions to this disappointing statistic are not only the texts we're assigning but also the ways we're approaching reading in schools—how we design courses, select texts, and think about literacy. We seek to create lifelong readers, yet we often focus more on the texts than we do on the readers. If students are not even reading the texts we assign (a looming turquoise giraffe in the room), then the *text*-centered, canonical-worshipping focus in many English language arts classrooms is obviously not working. The student who simply can't go to college without having read *The Great Gatsby*? Most likely, the student never even read the book when we assigned it.

In acknowledgment of this issue, the National Council of Teachers of English (NCTE) has published the position statement *Preparing Teachers with Knowledge of Children's and Young Adult Literature* (2018; the statement is reprinted in full in the front matter), which calls for more equitable approaches to text selection, instruction, and curriculum by introducing texts and instructional practices that allow adolescents to experience "windows, mirrors, and sliding glass doors" through their reading (Bishop, 1990). With more diverse texts, students can see aspects and reflections of themselves and their own worlds, look into worlds unfamiliar to them, and step into the worlds that authors create. Stephanie Toliver (2021) recently expanded on Bishop's metaphor by calling for "telescopes." She writes, "Through telescopes, children—especially those whose access to futures and fantasies has been distorted by violence and oppression—will be able to see that those futuristic and fantastical landscapes are actually closer than they first appeared to be" (p. 30). Having access to diverse texts gives students opportunities to explore their own worlds, explore other worlds, and imagine futures as they connect to their own realities.

Why YA Literature?

Before delving into how we can co-design courses with students, I want to share more about why young adult literature is so central to this approach. Although I recognize that texts should be one of the last elements of the course design process (we should first consider enduring understandings, essential questions, and assessment), the right texts can naturally inspire meaningful course design. YA literature in particular offers powerful opportunities for co-designed courses because it often forwards topics and social issues that are meaningful to students' lives, communities, and world. It offers opportunities for centering community within the classroom and leveraging community outside of the classroom.

Traditionally, the intended audience for young adult literature is adolescents in the secondary grades, or ages twelve to eighteen (Crowe, 1998). Since the inception of the field, however, the definition of *young adults* has expanded in both directions, to an age as low as ten and as high as twenty-five. Partly, this is because publishers might be stretching the target audience demographic to increase sales. In addition, due to the publication of books in the 1990s that were not easily classified and could serve as "crossovers" into adult fiction, the age boundaries extended even further (Cart, 2001, p. 95). Some researchers limit the category of YA titles to those books originally intended for an adolescent audience, but the issue is more complex than that: many preteens and teens are drawn to contemporary adult titles, and not all YA authors set out to write for this age of reader (Stephens, 2007). Although for convenience and a common understanding I am operating here under the traditional concept of a YA audience, we must acknowledge there are readers younger than twelve and older than eighteen who are drawn to YA literature, you and me included. Thinking about the age span for YA literature is important, though, because there is value in connecting students to books that feature protagonists who are similar to them in age. As readers inhabit worlds that reflect shared experiences or times in life, an iterative process of looking in to look out is set into motion.

Those who regularly read young adult literature understand that it holds the same potential for literary analysis as the best of adult literature and features complex, literary themes comparable to those revered in canonical texts. It offers opportunities for students to respond just as deeply and critically to strong YA literature as with classic literature (Buehler, 2016; Groenke & Scherff, 2010). Just because books are enjoyable or accessible to readers doesn't mean their content is neither difficult nor challenging (Ostenson & Wadham, 2012). Many YA books are indeed complex, and they have the advantage of offering both an accessibility that canonical literature often fails to provide (Brown & Mitchell, 2014) and the ability to "spark personal and social transformation" (NCTE 2018). In other words, a canonically based curriculum is not superior academically. Many adults buy novels intended for young adult readers and are pleasantly surprised to learn that these books have universal themes, include complex subject matter, and are genuinely engaging (Benedetti, 2011). Young adult texts can be powerfully transformative and thought-provoking. And as the field is exploding (or has already exploded, given the increasing aisle space dedicated to YA literature in bookstores), the public is beginning to (if it hasn't already) recognize its merit.

The incorporation of YA literature into the curriculum has the potential to transform classroom communities. The NCTE position statement (2018) reminds us that these books have great power to "affirm lived experience, create empathy, catalyze conversations, and respect the questions, challenges, and emotions of childhood and adolescence" (xii; page numbers map to the statement reprinted in the front matter). The inclusion of YA literature through participatory pedagogical approaches can significantly shape the ways in which we connect readers in English language arts instruction with a variety of communities. Further, for my standardized test–focused audience, the students are actually reading the books, which improves reading skills and supports the development of lifelong readers who approach texts with care and joy.

Young adult literature can be used in the English classroom to foster rich and deep analyses of literary texts in a process that parallels the instruction students experience through a classics-based curriculum. By reading and reflecting on a YA title, students can, for instance, examine theme and character and the arc of the story, define an author's audience and purpose, and evaluate how well figurative language, narrative structure, and symbolic reference create particular effects, just as they would in response to any other text. Because the field offers educators high-quality titles that attend to matters of consequence for preteen and teen readers, using these engaging texts to teach analytical skills has the potential to make lessons and assessment more memorable, authentic, and meaningful. The rewards of this kind of teaching are significant because students interact deeply with text. Young adult literature offers powerful potential for young people, who deserve to engage with texts intended specifically for them.

High-quality YA titles offer ample opportunity to teach analytical skills in the examination of literature. The best YA authors trust in their readers' willingness and ability to think beyond the words on the page and to craft interpretations grounded in careful examination of technique. If our goal is to help students learn to understand, contemplate, and question what they read, drawing on texts that appeal to these students is more likely to deliver the desired results.

Research repeatedly demonstrates that giving adolescents access to relatable texts that respect the experiences and challenges they will face leads to greater reader investment and interest (Buehler, 2016). From realistic fiction to fantasy, poetry to short stories, humor to mystery, traditional forms to more experimental forms, young adult fiction offers a wide array of reading options. These books allow us to think about how we craft our stories and how we share truth. Inviting readers to self-select at least some texts increases engagement in reading, and the more students read, the better readers they become (Fisher & Frey, 2012; Kelley et al., 2012; Moeller et al., 2011).

In the following chapters, I explore how courses that are co-designed with students and focused on community engagement can leverage young adult literature. The examples of assessment are authentic because they are connected to the students' school, local, and global communities. Students are positioned as lifelong readers and *thinkers*, and they are treated as real readers who use texts to engage in meaningful interactions as active members of their communities. These meaningful connections inspired by texts will simultaneously encourage persistence, stamina, and rich meaning-making as students read—much more so than an open-ended test or an essay designed by the teacher.

Limitations of YA Literature

Although I believe strongly in the power of young adult literature, I also recognize its limitations: particularly that it is most often written by adults and grounded in assumptions about adolescence/ts. For a deep discussion about this topic, I recommend exploring Robert Petrone, Sophia Tatiana Sarigianides, and Mark A. Lewis's (2015) theory related to the Youth Lens, which will allow you and your students to scrutinize how adolescence/ts are portrayed in young adult literature. When we do use YA lit in our classrooms, it's important to analyze how adolescence/ts are represented, what the dominant ideas about adolescence are, and the ways in which the text reinforces and/or subverts these ideas (p. 511).

Ideally, we would be able to feature texts written for adolescents by adolescents in our classrooms. Students would design their learning experiences using texts written by other teens who are able to share experiences and perspectives. However, students can work toward subverting the reality that most YA books are written by adults, both by using the Youth Lens to analyze texts and elevating and amplifying their own and one another's voices in their practice. They can consider how YA literature, as a tool, comes with its own limitations.

As a theory, the Youth Lens aligns in many ways with the major thrust of this book as I work to complicate assumptions about adolescents' place in the course design process and trust them to guide their own educational experiences. Through this empowerment and liberation from traditional curricula, they might choose to critique the dominant ways in which they are positioned, first in young adult literature and then within schools and other institutions.

It's Bigger Than Texts: Well-Read Students, Well-Informed Acts as Community Members

Offering a wide selection of texts can be transformative for students, but we must also consider *how* we are teaching these texts. Young adult texts shouldn't, for instance, be relegated to classroom libraries or taught in ways that perpetuate stereotypes. The NCTE position statement (2018) addresses issues critical to education—not just how we prepare to integrate YA lit but also how we think about the skills and strategies we value and the ways we "affirm diversity and exercise critical literacy" (xv). *Which* texts we are using is an important consideration, but the pedagogical strategies and approaches we implement require perhaps a more critical conversation.

But before we can even think about which texts we are using or the pedagogical approaches to instruction, we must first consider the epistemologies that inform how we view teaching and schools and how we demonstrate our trust in students to be agents of their own learning experiences. The ways we think about how knowledge is produced in classrooms and our framing of education, thinking, and learning drive everything we do as teachers, including our text selection processes and pedagogical approaches. If we believe that young adult literature is a meaningful factor that can engage students in reading and improving their reading habits, practices, and/or skills and allow for connections with our school, local, and global communities, we must first think about how our classrooms and courses are designed to center students' and communities' thinking, interests, and needs before we even think about which specific texts we will use. So let's pause to consider how our epistemological beliefs can guide us to leverage student voices, expertise, experiences, and interests in order to position them as knowledge producers who have a part to play in the course design process.

Rethinking Conceptions of Community and Inquiry in the Classroom

As a child, I quickly came to understand that schools were not aligned with my own cultural beliefs and lifeways. My community and relatives valued consensus building, a concept that is largely ignored in the ways schools are structured and courses are designed. In my years as a teacher, I have worked to imagine how schools and classrooms could be consensus-building spaces in which student and community interests are central to course design.

Here's what grounds my own teaching: Students aren't empty piggy banks to be filled with the teachers' coins of knowledge through lectures and teacher-directed instruction (Freire, 2000). Engaged learning requires active participation in social communities and a focus on maximizing our learning about ourselves, in community and with community. For us as educators to truly integrate students' funds of knowledge into our classrooms (Moll et al., 1992), we must design courses *with* students, and problem-posing inquiry should be at the forefront of curricular design (Freire, 2000). In other words, classrooms committed to engagement with school, local, and global communities must place students' funds of knowledge, passions, interests, and goals at the center of course design. Without a co-designed format, too often we are focused on our own personal interests and goals rather than those of our students.

Community shouldn't merely be the result or end goal of a valued class experience— community should exist as action. It should be repositioned as a verb—an actively driving principle that influences everything that occurs in a classroom. Students shouldn't merely be heard in the process—they should be trusted as curriculum designers and instructional architects. One of the epistemological perspectives that drives my thinking is Wenger's (1999) conception of communities of practice. Wenger reminds us that, although we are social beings, classrooms and schools are currently designed under the assumption that we learn best as *individuals* rather than in community and through collaboration. The knowledge taught in schools too often seems to exist as pieces of information that we store in our individual brains. A "smart" individual is one who can spew back *Jeopardy*-style facts as disconnected bits of information. When we examine a curriculum, these bits and pieces of knowledge are divided into disparate instructional units or matched with standards to be housed among instructional units.

These assumptions, Wenger (1999) points out, are then accompanied with behavioral-based grading systems and classroom management strategies that attempt to remove distractions from a student's *individual* intake of information. High-stakes tests, which currently matter most in the vast majority of districts, are individualized, proctored, and silent, and in most testing situations, collaboration is penalized as cheating.

Even when we consider building communities in classrooms, we usually think about how community emerges as the *result* or at the end of a powerful learning space, rather than positioning community as the starting place for course design. We might, for example, see some echoes of Wenger's communities of practice dotting classrooms in end-of-semester group or civic engagement projects. In contrast, I envision secondary English classroom communities of practice differently—as privileged at the very beginning of a school experience in both course design and structures. I envision classroom spaces where we trust students to craft their curriculum from the very first day.

But I want to step back for a moment to really define and explain communities of practice and connect the concept to classrooms. A community of practice is a group of people who seek to deepen their understanding, knowledge, and expertise about a shared concern, problem, or passion. More specifically, they meet on an ongoing basis to hold discussions, share information and aspirations, explore ideas, and offer insight and advice (Wenger et al., 2002). We see and participate in communities all the time, but not all of them can be classified as communities of practice. As Wenger (1999) describes, a neighborhood is a community but not (typically) a community of practice. Or sometimes individuals come together briefly or temporarily to draft a document, as practice, but they are not a community. A true community of practice is a group of people who engage in both *participation* and *reification* (practice).

Communities of practice are not a new concept to the literacy space. For instance, Skerrett et al. (2018) used Wenger's conception of communities of practice to identify and theorize professional learning opportunities and professional development for their teacher participants that "promoted or constrained their development as equity-oriented teachers" (p. 120). Here, I apply the theory not to teachers, but instead to the group of students in a classroom setting.

Each member of the community brings different experiences from previous settings and different values, so everyone doesn't have to hold identical ideals; instead, each member brings a set of experiences that help work toward "sustained pursuit of a shared enterprise" (Wenger, 1999, p. 45). A community of practice evolves with each shared pursuit. Students find mutuality with one another and are also able to recognize themselves within each other. Participation enables all members of the community to learn, and this learning will change each member of the community. The experience of community alone can allow for learning beyond what might be expected in a particular setting—in other words, students might learn literacy skills, as expected, but they might also gain knowledge about how to be stronger activists and how to engage more powerfully in their communities.

As a community of practice engages in participation, it is also critical to their purpose and membership that they engage in *reification*, or practice (Wenger, 1999). A classroom isn't a community of practice if students are just forming positive relationships, encouraging each other, and building bridges together. Their work must extend beyond the classroom. The reification process might include "making, designing, representing, naming, encoding and describing as well as perceiving, interpreting, using, reusing, decoding and recasting" (Wenger, 1999, pp. 58–59). There must be a balance—community members must have time to "share experience and interactive negotiation" (p. 65) (participation), but they must also produce artifacts in some form to engage with the world outside of the classroom and situate themselves within authentic spaces (reification). A classroom community of practice can't just hang out and discuss and make meaning together, and alternatively, they can't be solely focused on external output. Both participation and reification must occur and be valued. In Chapters 3 and 4, I offer examples from real classrooms that demonstrate participation, reification, and the ways in which the two interact.

Communities of practice concepts are parallel to contemporary, equity-oriented, youth-centered, and community-centered theories and approaches within education, such as youth participatory action research (see, for instance,

Cammarota & Fine, 2008; McIntyre, 2000) and culturally sustaining pedagogies (Paris & Alim, 2017, appendix). By a strict definition of Wenger's concept, true communities of practice would loop within the school, as some former students would continue in the community when new members were integrated in the school. In the real world, however, school semesters are typically divided into distinct points of time and the school year is traditionally nine months long. Therefore, although it would be powerful to design a school that breaks away from the traditional semester structure to support a true definition of an evolving, more indefinite community of practice, in this book I share approaches that are a bit closer to our current reality. The major goal of this approach—purposeful spaces for participation and reification—is the core of this book, mining the pedagogical opportunities of connected, student-designed spaces.

What to Expect in This Book

This book is designed to move away from teacher-directed curricula and instead move toward curricular design that is community-based and co-facilitated with students. It includes approaches that I and other teachers have used to frame these discussions with students in order to develop community-based, student-generated classroom design. We use young adult literature as a potential tool (but not a magic ticket) for engaging in social issues and designing experiences and *practice* that create and leverage community. Chapter 2 offers further background on communities of practice and provides a heuristic for enacting a co-designed community of practice model. Specifically, I outline the general steps for building a community of practice: developing a domain, building and maintaining a community, and establishing practice. The concepts of this chapter are then threaded through the remaining chapters with specific classroom examples.

Chapters 3 and 4 respond directly to the NCTE (2018) position statement's call for teachers to use appropriate pedagogy. Both describe explicitly how the ideas in Chapter 2 might be enacted in the classroom—through student-designed, co-generated communities of practice. In Chapter 3, I use the metaphor of rattling a cage to think about how we might break down the bars of existing, often hegemonic and rigid course structures to infuse young adult literature into existing courses. This chapter attends to the curricular and organizational limitations often found in schools and provides multiple models of how we can co-generate spaces and how YA literature might be incorporated into all communities—regardless of the setting in which you and your students work. Chapter 4 uses the metaphor of hands to describe how students and others can help harness the potential of young adult literature to (re)design a stand-alone course. This chapter posits that course design and instruction should include and involve students to allow for critical freedom and voice. I share several approaches to thinking about these courses, along with ideas that are adaptable to both teacher and student needs. I detail the process from start to finish, beginning with a description of how to draft a course proposal and how to introduce and justify the idea to colleagues and leaders within a school community. Additionally, I address logistical concerns that come with the creation of a new course, such as getting the necessary books and other materials, setting up the classroom and classroom library, soliciting students for the course, and assessing student progress.

In Chapter 5, I offer suggestions for how we can lead literate lives and join the community of readers in our classrooms. Included are suggestions about how to better know the literature and what's behind the books (e.g., scholarship, reviews) and how to connect with authors, colleagues, and others in the field. With this knowledge, we can engage in the participatory practices described in this chapter to create community in our classrooms and leverage community locally, globally, and with technology.

Finally, the annotated bibliography offers suggestions of texts that have framed my own thinking and that I recommend if you're interested in gathering a holistic conception of how, why, and what we teach and with which framings, approaches, and practices we might use as we envision ourselves as co-designers with students. I recommend sharing these resources with students, too, as they engage in course design. This book cannot exist alone, and it exists only because of the work of others who came before me. And for their work, I am grateful.

Chapter Two

Steps for Enacting Communities of Practice in the Classroom

Sharing control of curriculum design with students takes courage. It can feel terrifying, chaotic, and uncomfortable, but allowing students to become course designers alongside us reminds them that they are valued and important enough to design their own learning experiences. As teachers, we are able to learn and grow too in community as each of our classes includes a different set of students with a different set of interests, perspectives, and ideas. To an outsider, this design approach might appear to be less work for teachers (less teacher-directed lesson planning, for instance). But it is actually often more work because we must consider daily how to best act as stewards as students co-design their class experience together. This is hard but meaningful work, and it is the kind of work that can sustain us as educators as we watch the process evolve and support members of our communities of practice.

As emphasized in the NCTE position statement (2018), pedagogical approaches must affirm diversity and exercise critical literacy. Literacy instruction cannot occur in a vacuum. It must be humanizing for the young people inside (and outside) of our classrooms. In classrooms that exercise critical literacy, students not only work in communities but also engage with their communities locally and globally, and equity, diversity, and inclusion frame this work. Butler and colleagues (2020) write about how a grounding in social justice must "come to name oppressive ideologies, challenge unfair educational practices, and dismantle inequitable structures" (p. 91), and we must move from fear and focus on our responsibility to humanize classroom spaces. Classrooms can be centered as sites for powerful inquiry that *matter* to students; these might include critically literate approaches in which students are working toward linguistic, racial, and social justice (Baker-Bell, 2020; Baker-Bell et al., 2017; Borsheim-Black & Sarigianides, 2019). But before students engage with real issues that are relevant to themselves and their school, local, and global communities, we must first think about the communities we are building *inside* of the classroom and how we can engage these spaces in participatory ways.

In this chapter, I focus on the specific elements that define a community of practice and then share how those elements took shape in a secondary classroom I taught, an elective young adult literature course. As you read, I hope that you might think about how these elements might impact your own teaching.

Elements of a Community of Practice

According to Wenger et al. (2002), communities of practice are guided by three elements that exist concurrently: domain, community, and practice. These elements are determined by the participants (in our case, the students) along with the teachers, who intentionally work to reduce themselves from positions of power to serving in a managerial role as a steward. As a steward, I seek to offer students learning opportunities as needed and to regularly push them to think more deeply, as needed. In the classroom community of practice, my goal is to step back and observe as much as possible as students increasingly push one another to think more deeply. I work intentionally to serve as a member of the community of practice, offering text ideas but avoiding telling students how to use those texts.

Domain

In the very beginning days of a classroom experience that centers the idea of a community of practice, students can start by discussing the topics or issues they care about and that are relevant to their school, local, and global communities. For a school focus, the class might bring in other students, teachers, or administrators within or across departments. For a local focus, this might involve bringing in community members from local organizations and councils. And for a global focus, the class might bring in or connect with global leaders or even utilize TED talks, videos, and podcasts of those who speak on a variety of global issues. Students can help identify the people they feel will contribute to their thinking about their local, school, and global issues. Whatever the focus and interest, Wenger reminds us that "communities of practice are not contained entities. They develop in larger contexts—historical, social, cultural, institutional—with specific resources and constraints" and they respond with agency "to their conditions, and therefore, their enterprise" (1999, p. 80). The students' inquiry should be engaged with the world outside of the classroom in authentic ways, and the questions and answers they seek should not arise from the teacher's interests but rather from their own, shifting with the learning of the classroom as interests evolve. These topics students choose to focus on constitute the *domains* of a community of practice.

One move that I, as the steward of the classroom, have made to help facilitate this conversation is to ask students how they might "read the world" (Freire, 1985). This question inspires students to think about issues that matter to them, and it aligns with Vasquez's (2017) concept of critical literacy, in which students are invited to share interests, experiences, and artifacts as they engage critically and thoughtfully with their world as a way of being, living, and learning (Pandya & Ávila, 2014; Vasquez et al., 2019), building significance in their lives. Most often, critical literacy is examined through lenses of oppression and privilege (Luke, 2000). As an example, our class might ask family, friends, and community members about instances of injustice in their communities. They might then develop these ideas into topics for research and read young adult literature and other resources about the topics. They can then connect their topics and identify actual elements in their communities they want to change, and then begin to work toward this change, rather than simply talking about it in a discussion circle.

Our curiosities, interests, and identified domains within community partnerships should create a place of exchange in which we learn, in dialogue, with our communities. In other words, a community should be positioned for its rich potential and possibilities for collaborative learning and growth. Communities of practice merge with critical literacy in that the domains students choose to study in community develop organically through inquiry on the very first day the students enter the classroom (Vasquez, 2017), and their topics most often connect with issues of equity, diversity, inclusion, and justice.

To identify the primary domain to be studied, students might begin by writing a list of open-ended questions they care deeply about. I also encourage them to have discussions with family, friends, and community members to help develop these questions. If students are younger and inquiry questions are too difficult, they might begin with topics they are interested in exploring. Here, we can serve as stewards by asking them to share topics they would be interested in exploring in their communities and the ways in which they can connect their classroom spaces with their communities. Sometimes my students brainstorm as a group and select a topic we all care deeply about, and then we identify our roles in this space. Students define their own responsibilities for the group and how they will contribute to aspects of the research process they then develop collaboratively. Other times, we select an overarching topic of interest, like justice, and each student or group of students selects a subtopic to explore, perhaps racial or environmental justice. We can loosely explore options for practice during the brainstorming session for our domain, but these often evolve as we learn and read more and invite in community partners. It can be difficult to define how we might participate in our school, local, and/or global communities before we have a strong grasp of the state of affairs and needs within the domain.

Community

As described in Chapter 1, you can work to foster community intentionally from the very first day your class meets, but a community naturally builds and grows with each encounter. A community must be nurtured, with careful attention to each student's role, expertise, interests, and perspectives (Wenger et al., 2002), and a community of practice is wise to explicitly identify these roles, expectations for connections, and ways they might intentionally use their energy to build trust among members. As stewards, we need to explicitly and regularly encourage students to think metacognitively about their community of practice. If tensions arise, for instance, the students might discuss what is working and what is not working in their classroom.

Building Ethical and Professional Norms within our Communities of Practice

As we consider our community of practice in this metacognitive way, it's important to establish a shared set of norms. Campano et al.'s (2015) discussion of professional and ethical norms in community-based research specifically focuses on how researchers can foster trust in "contexts of cultural diversity, systemic inequity, and power asymmetry" (p. 30). The collaborations they discuss specifically refer to those in which there is a power differential between researchers and communities—which, in some ways, can compare to some of the power differentials we see in schools between teachers and students. Their work is particularly relevant for teachers who work in culturally diverse schools with students who have historically been disempowered by a variety of systems, including educational systems. We would *all*, regardless of our placements, benefit from thinking about power differentials and how Campano and colleagues' conceptions of norms are relevant to student-centered teaching as we develop shared visions of social, cultural, linguistic, and institutional boundaries in our literacy practices and discourses.

In a true community of practice, norms are continually evolving and dynamic as the group's interests develop and change with ongoing participation. A classroom community of practice is engaged externally, not limited to the four walls of the classroom. This community is engaged in *real change* and requires theoretical and practical knowledge in order to move forward successfully. Campano et al. also state that norms must not only be real but also be ethical. Classroom communities of practice must extend beyond self-interest to look specifically at our engagement together and with others—to examine how our contexts are situated with each other and the world. There must be a "self-reflexive component throughout every stage of the inquiry process, which entails participants considering how they may be superimposing and universalizing their own principles and interests onto others" (p. 34).

Thus, our communities of practice must be reflexive about their own interests and principles and how these extend beyond the individual and the communities of practice themselves. Members—and especially the teacher—must consistently consider how they are considering others' perspectives, interests, and concerns. We can be self-reflexive about how our interests are impacting the community and the ways we are intentionally bringing in other points of view. A community of practice thinks carefully about community contexts and connections.

Campano et al. (2015) worked in a university-community partnership, developing a set of professional and ethical norms that they understood would evolve and change dynamically. These norms are specific to their partnership, yet they offer fodder and grounding for how we might work with students to develop our own set of norms in communities of practice that demonstrate mutual trust. Like Wenger's (1999) theory of communities of practice, Campano and colleagues don't expect that this mutual trust necessitates that all members share the same perspectives and interests. Although participants may share a common sense of identity, a community of practice is celebrated for the diverse viewpoints, skills, and positions of its members. Disagreements might, instead, be sites of inquiry. Although these norms are attached to a specific school site, they remind readers that they are not meant to be prescriptive; their norms should not be *our* community of practice's norms. Instead, we can learn from them and share them with students to facilitate conversations about norms in our own spaces.

Within our community of practice, everyone must be treated as contributors to the group, and all members should be valued for their capacity and strength to lead initiatives (Campano et al., 2015). A small group of students might, for instance, solicit feedback from other members of the community of practice and work to ensure transparency. They might also report back to us, as teachers, on ways we can move away from a hierarchical power structure in the classroom space. This group might include other members of the school community and the local community, creating a fluid, engaged conversation and feedback loop.

Building a place of trust is imperative in this work, and in order for students to know one another, we must work with them to consider how they might facilitate and co-create a space where they come to understand and respect everyone's perspective and where everyone feels a sense of belonging. So students might co-design classroom norms and share expectations for a course. They might develop both personal and shared goals for learning together. Obviously, we as teachers bring a set of experiential knowledge and expertise to the classroom, but we should intentionally position ourselves as stewards of knowledge (Wenger et al., 2002) rather than teachers in power.

Acting as stewards can be difficult for us. It means that we must not direct the activities so much as support them. We might ask students, for instance, "How can we develop a shared set of expectations for our space? How might we document those expectations? What options do we have available to us?" This means that we don't come in with a set idea and have students write a contract on poster board and sign it. The students will instead determine how and in what way they will demonstrate their beliefs and expectations for the community of practice. The teacher, as steward, is a manager who participates in the process and engages their expertise in an active process, so it's critical that they have a storehouse of knowledge (Wenger et al., 2002). Given the context of this book, for example, we teachers must have expertise in young adult literature (see Chapter 5 for more about how teachers might engage in the literary world) and have a strong set of ideas and practices to share with students as potential opportunities for learning (see Chapters 3, 4, and 5 for pedagogical approaches and participatory practices).

Every community of practice must implement an explicit knowledge strategy through a concrete strategic plan. Members co-determine how they will develop and apply their capabilities in order to execute their strategy. Although they may produce documents or specific practices of their knowledge, more valuable is the ways in which a community of practice is a living repository for their collective knowledge (Wenger et al., 2002).

Practice

A community of practice is organized to allow members to share insight, aspirations, situations, information, and advice as they work together to solve problems. Critical reading and conversation alone don't constitute critical literacy, so this approach must include contemporary social topics and committed social action

(Wolfe, 2010). As mentioned earlier, key to our communities of practice is reification: members engage intentionally and systematically in the management of their knowledge and participate in *practice*. They might create tools, documents, standards, or other artifacts, and this reification is designed to be shared (Wenger et al., 2002).

Over time a community of practice must move beyond discussing and studying their *domain* and examining their roles within their *community*. They need to engage in a form of *practice*, and it should be outward-facing, not isolated in the classroom. Students determine the knowledge they wish to share, develop, or document. The community of practice works together to build a unit that ends with a solid, outward-facing product. Once the students have identified a domain, they can consider how they want to be assessed (or what they will produce, as *practice*, to demonstrate their knowledge), and then they can determine learning activities and texts that will help lead them to informed assessments of their knowledge. Their practice might be a large collaborative project, in which each student has a co-determined role, or it might feature smaller projects among groups or independent projects related to the domain and community-defined needs.

The communities of practice in my classes have typically chosen to engage in practice that promotes literacy in their school and local communities and to engage with social issues locally or globally. Campano et al.'s (2015) final norm reiterates that *research must be public and be shared transparently, collaboratively, and creatively*. Throughout this book, I share examples of what this kind of practice might look like for your communities of practice and how you can work alongside students as they engage transparently, collaboratively, and creatively in their communities. Their practice doesn't emerge from a project list or a choice of writing prompts that you define or provide. Instead, this practice is developed after significant collaboration and discussion with students who make meaning from their shared goals for their work.

Example of a Community of Practice in Action

Let's take a look at how theories of communities of practice intersect with critical literacy and take form in actual classrooms. On the very first day of our classes, we can focus on these more democratic ways of "being and doing" to create critically literate classrooms that support our students' passions (Vasquez et al., 2019). On day one of a young adult literature elective class I taught, for example, students began by sharing why they had joined the YA literature elective. Several students noted that they had enrolled because they were tired of being told what to read in school. They talked further about the concept of the freedom to read, and during this discussion, we determined that this idea could and would drive our design of the first unit—a unit now centered on their interests. As steward, I asked them to develop inquiry questions related to this *domain*—questions they wanted answered. Some of the questions they brainstormed included:

- Who decides what we read?
- How do schools, libraries, and bookstores influence what we read?
- How does censorship impact schools?
- What counts as reading?

Once we had developed our domain for exploration, we were able to consider our *community*. Students volunteered the ways in which they could bring their knowledge, skills, and strengths to the exploration of these inquiry questions. We considered how we, as a community, could join in a shared learning experience and how we could connect with our local community as we did so. Together, we designed our unit of instruction, which we knew would be dynamic as we studied their inquiry questions.

Next, students designed the end-of-unit assessment, or the *practice* aspect of our communities of practice. Obviously, my students didn't have experience developing an instructional unit. As steward, I shared with them that the first step in designing an instructional unit is addressing the big questions they'd already developed. I encouraged them to use these questions to think about the practice, or the end goal of their unit. During our first brainstorming sessions, the students said they wanted the unit to culminate with letters to the English teachers, administration, and Board of Education in their school community about their thoughts on canonical texts. They wanted to write to the Board of Education specifically to speak back to the strict policy regarding texts (they were angry that R-rated movies weren't allowed in the schools, for instance). They also wanted to write a public letter with an attached petition about how censorship harmed their intellectual freedom. They intended to write a collection of letters, groups of students taking the lead on research and engaging in writers workshop to offer input on every letter they sent.

Engaging in a community of practice requires us to be flexible. As students expressed interests related to our domain and the four primary inquiry questions they had developed, we identified content that would help us learn more. During the unit, we:

- studied how schools, libraries, and bookstores influence which texts we read;
- read about review systems that impact the books that librarians, teachers, and bookstore owners purchase for course texts;
- visited a bookstore and asked questions (more on this in Chapter 4);

- divided into book groups that each read a commonly banned book and researched letters from parents and schools that banned these books;
- looked at censorship statistics and read documents on the NCTE Intellectual Freedom Center website;
- participated in Banned Books Week on social media;
- read articles about the different ways they might reconsider what counts as reading; and
- joined in shared conversation throughout each of these learning experiences and referred back to our inquiry questions to determine regularly how we might learn more and advance our dialogue and contribution to our local community.

Throughout the process, I offered some of the participatory practices shared in Chapters 4 and 5 to allow the students to engage in independent reading and sharing practices. These activities provided students with confidence in their ability to talk about the power of young adult literature and the freedom to read. At the end of this unit, the students determined that writing letters, as a form of *practice*, wasn't enough. Ultimately, the practice they engaged in evolved from the letters they had initially conceived in their original course design. They decided that they wanted to develop a knowledge repository. This allowed them to write the letters they had originally intended (which they also sent), but they also designed informational pages for peers in other classes, posters for Banned Books Week, justifications for including controversial texts in their classes, and suggestions for more equitable text selection practices for their school library. They organized a meeting with key community partners, such as the local librarian, school librarian, and children's book manager at the local bookstore, and they also wrote a proposal for a new district censorship policy.

I share this student-designed classroom unit to demonstrate how the students, who on the first day shared that they were "tired of being told what to read" and angry at the limits placed on their intellectual freedom, developed a *domain* driven by inquiry questions they cared deeply about. They then drafted end goals (letters) of *practice*, which shifted as they learned more. And we regularly checked in on and metacognitively discussed how our *community* was developing during this first unit and shared feedback on the ways we could improve our community of practice. We were a community that existed within the context of a larger community. We had many opportunities for participation, but we also engaged in a form of reification to connect with the broader community.

When we participate in a true community of practice, our lesson plans must be written in pencil. We walk in with plans for facilitating conversation based on the students' interests, and these plans evolve with the community of practice's interests. For instance, you might know that each book group is reading a text that has been commonly censored. Rather than designing discussion questions or guided thinking, you might say to the class, "What is our domain? What are the inquiry questions we might develop that are meaningful to us and our local and/or global community? How does reading these texts help us think deeply about our domain and inquiry questions? How might we learn more? What questions should we be asking ourselves?" This then leads to an organic process in which students determine the next steps for their unit with your guidance, as needed. If your school or district requires you to teach directly to standards, define your domain, community, and practice first. Then you can analyze the standards alongside students to determine how they can research their domain while still addressing the standards. At the end of each session, you can talk about next steps for the following class day, so the agenda for each day is communally driven and students coauthor the lesson plans (and you flesh out the details for school accountability purposes). The students map their own learning, and your job as steward is to support the students as leaders of their own learning.

In a community of practice, students are invited to shift the learning to meet their needs. As a teacher, this is exciting because one comment can change the entire course of a unit. For instance, if this same set of inquiry questions emerged again today, in 2022, I might point students to a recently published young adult book related to censorship called *You Can't Say That! Writers for Young People Talk about Censorship, Free Expression, and the Stories They Have to Tell* (Marcus, 2021). I might ask them how they could leverage this book in their understanding of the domain. Their interests might shift the direction of our unit. Perhaps they wouldn't be interested in the text at all, and we would search for another or several texts to be read in book groups. Or maybe a student would express interest in thinking about their own stories and the moments they have been censored. This might shift us to a discussion of the power of story, and perhaps students would decide that writing personal narratives related to censorship and sharing them on a local radio station or as podcasts or TED-like talks would be the way they wanted to engage in practice. Each member of the community of practice contributes to the ways in which we engage together and learn, and discussing the students' interests will shift the assessment, or the practice.

Example of a Community of Practice with Multiple Domains

A community of practice can act in solidarity as members critically consider and engage with their world while undertaking different projects. As students consider what is meaningful learning for them, their community, and their lives, they might identify different domains they are interested in exploring. Once each student or groups of students identifies domains of interest, the teacher steward might, for instance, share a variety of critical frameworks, theories, or approaches that students can use as lenses to view their different domains of interest. Wendy Glenn and I (2019) explore the potential of using critical lenses and approaches for analyzing young adult literature and the world, such as positioning theory; the social mind; neoliberalism; the dominant/oppositional gaze; multiethnic/multicultural/multiracial alloys; borders and borderlands; racial melancholia; interrogations of happiness; queer reading practices and ideologies; complications of the coming out story; theories of space, place, and navigational identity; interrogating historical violence; critical race English education; critical language awareness; critical comparative content analysis; deconstructions of the superhero; arts-based approaches for social justice; and Afrofuturism. I list all of these critical approaches and theories here intentionally to highlight the endless possibilities for students to use critical theories and approaches to think deeply about their domains of interest.

Whatever the critical perspective, approach, or theory, students should have the opportunity and space to check in and share their learning in *community* and take action, in *practice*, with regard to the policies and practices that impact their lives and the communities outside of their classroom. One student, for instance, might investigate neoliberalism in city policies and read a text that offers insight into this thinking. That student might attend a city meeting to speak in the public open forum. Alternatively, two students might both use a lens that critically analyzes language to explore two different texts of interest and to examine the ways in which language is taught in their school, and then advocate for new ways of thinking in their school community and at local sites. In this example, students take on different domains and explore the ways in which these domains can lead to practice within their communities.

In these two examples, I offer models that allow for collective and individual exploration, in which we trust students to develop their own inquiry questions, engage in social issues, and analyze the ways in which power is structured in invisible and visible ways in classrooms and communities. They engage collaboratively in critically literate approaches designed intentionally to empower them in their everyday world (Lee & Schoonover, 2020; Vasquez et al., 2019). Literacy is a vehicle for transformative change, and students are invited to drive the vehicle as engaged critical agents. This approach offers great potential for involving students in community and in response to community as they work to enact social change, and it seeks to empower all students, but specifically underserved youth (Lee & Schoonover, 2020; Morrell, 2008), such as those who were enrolled in my YA lit course discussed earlier.

Conclusion

A community of practice relies on three elements: a *domain* that students define collaboratively, regular monitoring of the *community* and the contributions and strengths of those in it, and the development of a form of *practice* to share our collaborative efforts with others. We must act as stewards to guide this process and be willing to embrace the messiness of co-generative design. This requires us to position ourselves as learners who are willing to shift instruction and goals day to day and week to week to highlight the innovation that regularly occurs in our classroom communities of practice and that reflects the dynamic interests and needs of the students in our communities. In the following chapter, I share the ways this approach can be integrated into existing, rigid, and/or traditional course designs and requirements. Then, in Chapter 4, I share a structure of what this approach might look like in a young adult literature elective, one that is free from some of the rigidity that often accompanies traditional courses. The final chapter shares examples of how we can lead literate lives and join our community of readers in our classrooms.

Chapter Three

Rattling the Cage of Existing and/or More Rigid Courses

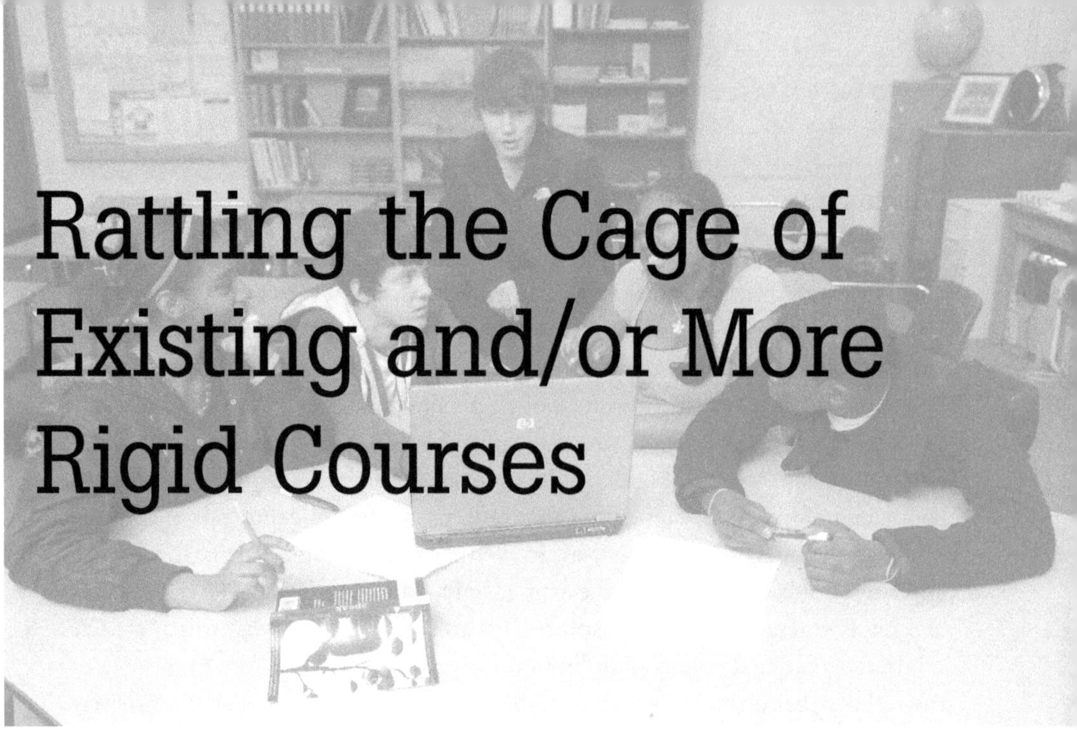

The first two chapters of this book explore the ways in which we might rethink our approaches to teaching by building a community of practice in which students come together to identify a domain, reflexively and dynamically adapt their community as they progress, and develop a practice together (Wenger et al., 2002). This chapter delves into how we might integrate these concepts into the ways we approach existing, rigid, and/or traditional course designs and curricular requirements in schools. In the pedagogical approaches described in this chapter, we invite students into the course design process by exploring the concepts of community of practice described in the previous chapters. In alignment with the NCTE position statement (2018), students are intentionally focusing pedagogy and integrating young adult literature to allow for "critical, significant conversations about their lives" (xvi) as they curate their own learning. In many of our teaching situations, we may be limited by curricula and structures and thus not creating true communities of practice, where students are fully taking the reins of the entire course framework. This chapter offers a way for you—if you work in one of these environments—to realistically adapt your classroom for greater flexibility. It offers a first step for those with more rigid curricula to move toward a truly student-designed curriculum. (See Chapter 4 for a more authentic conception of communities of practice at work in a more open, flexible school or course design structure.)

Rattling the Cage: A Metaphor

I invite you to consider a metaphor that urges you to rattle the cage. If the bars of the cage are existing school systems, consider what is trapped inside the bars with your students. Perhaps it is rigid curricular guidelines, a departmental value on teacher-centered instructional practices, standardized testing, canonical texts that you know your students aren't reading, a fifty-year-old vocabulary book that must be taught weekly, a grammar book that contains some sentence diagramming. What's in your cage?

Figure 3.1. A visual representation of the metaphor of rattling the cage.

Next, consider how you might rattle that cage harder than you've ever rattled it before. Figure 3.1 shares a visual diagram of cage rattling in which students—represented by the hands inside the cage—are a part of the process of breaking down, critiquing, and redesigning nonresponsive practices and rigid curricular approaches. You might be that hand outside the cage. You might be saying, "Enough is enough," and bringing in the beam of light if doing so ensures that students aren't placed in a vulnerable position that may cause them harm. Or maybe the hand that brings in light could be replaced by the hands of your students.

As you look at the figure, ask yourself: "What are the cage bars that interfere with my ability to teach in critical and responsive ways?" Take a moment to annotate the diagram to fit your school structure: What are the bars? What is inside and outside of the cage? Whose hands might help break down those bars?

Although ideally we would all exist in environments that allow for the freedom of students to co-generate their intellectual spaces completely, I have worked in enough secondary schools to know that rattling this cage may be incredibly difficult for you. The bars of the school system sometimes seem impenetrable, made of titanium cemented deeply into the ground. Maybe you are stuck with required courses encaged by the bars of a Board of Education, scripted curricula (with a literal script), and/or weekly observations policing your practices. Maybe you have parents who picket outside of your school building or loom in your classroom library, censoring at will. You might feel like you are outside of the cage and watching your students trapped inside. Even though *you* might feel ready, it might require a significant amount of care and precision to push instructional approaches and texts through the bars to break that cage down from the inside. Hegemony surrounds schools and courses in ways that are both visible and invisible, and sometimes it takes a conscious, concerted effort and years of labor to push aside the cage bars.

Yet I still invite you to rattle the cage—even if that cage feels like it will never break open. Find support in other colleagues and administrators and rattle the cage together. If you can't knock down the cage completely just yet and build a completely co-generated community of practice, then find the spaces between the bars to push in co-generative, community-based methods, approaches, and texts as much as you can as you work slowly to pry apart the bars until they collapse. If you see someone—a colleague, an administrator, a Board of Education member—who is applying more cement to the cage to keep the bars strong and rigid curricula inside, have a conversation, share student experiences, and use whatever means you have to interrupt the cement-laying until that old cement begins to crack and crumble. For some, it will take significant, focused effort, and they will have to slide texts between the bars in the middle of the night. They will start whispering about intellectual freedom and grow louder as their community builds. I feel firmly that any teacher who is willing can move toward the liberatory practices discussed in this book—it just might take longer and require significantly more effort and metalwork to cut through that titanium.

For other readers, the cage is made of paper, and all it needs is you and/or a school-level or local community with the willingness and readiness to take a pair of scissors to begin snipping the bars to build something new. The only limit here is your and your students' imaginations as you build something new together. You and your students can co-generate the entire course design and build a community of practice of your own creation (Chapter 4 explores the possibilities of this more flexible format).

Here, I offer suggestions and approaches for teachers who don't *yet* have the ability to build a true community of practice and who are seeking ways they might work toward a community of practice within existing structures. This chapter welcomes you to rattle the cage harder than ever before—to crack the cement around the cage and celebrate student successes and triumphs in intentional ways that result from their practices. It accommodates all teacher-readers, from those in the more rigid situations to those who have pushed apart some of the bars of their cage and have already begun this work. Regardless of where you and your school exist in a commitment to equity and your level of autonomy, there are opportunities for real change in our schools and classrooms that work toward building communities of practice. Teachers interested in and willing to infuse young adult literature into their courses, for instance, can do so in ways that support students and improve their skills in and attitudes toward reading.

In this chapter and the next, I describe multiple visions of how you might shift your approach away from traditional classroom structures while using YA literature. These range from modest changes to existing curricula (small items slipped through the bars of the cage) to practices that can result in radical (re)configurations of the classroom space and instructional practices.

I offer many examples related to one of the most impenetrable courses taught in secondary schools: American Literature. While many teachers feel confident rattling the cage for a variety of courses (ninth-grade English, tenth-grade English, etc.), they often step back from the cage as if it is electrified when it holds the contents of the revered American Literature course. Why is it that often teachers can envision space for YA literature in every course except American Literature? The history of the United States and a loyalty to the American Literature canon runs deep within schools. I ask you to step back from your nostalgia and positive memories—if you have any—of specific American literature texts that you read during your own schooling and envision the ways this course can be reimagined. We need to ask ourselves whose vision of the United States these canonical American Literature texts (and often the accompanying approaches to teaching these texts) validate and affirm and whose is not. Addressing this disconnect allows us to begin the work toward developing a community of practice.

To be clear, I am not advocating for removing the American Literature course from schools; instead, I am inviting you to work with students to reimagine the focus and purpose of this course, to consider which voices are honored as American in this course, and to think about how YA literature might strengthen the potential of this course for all students. As Muhammad (2020) writes, literacy offers us a criticality to examine and understand power, privilege, and oppression; historically responsive literacy embodies beliefs and practices that respond authentically to the cultures of students, the cultures of others, and the current and historical social times. (See the annotated bibliography for a fuller description of Muhammad's text.) In an American Literature course, students might define a domain that examines what it means to be an American, and they could identify different texts for analyzing this concept. They might look at historical and contemporary visions of being an American and examine these ideations in relation to their own lives and backgrounds. And then they could identify a way to share their learning as a community of practice by connecting their new knowledge with their school, local, or global community. This might, for instance, include sharing their histories and pushing back in a campaign against a local policy.

This chapter includes a wealth of examples of teachers who have centered their students in and integrated young adult literature into their existing, required (and often traditional) English courses. Not all of these teacher examples are focused on American Literature, but their contexts and curricula, which vary greatly, allow for a wider look at applications to other courses as well. I want to note that each of these teachers was under varying degrees of influence and expectations within their school systems. Some of their contexts might be more rigid or more flexible than your own, and they are intended to serve as inspiration for adaptability for you and your students. Of primary importance in the approaches here and elsewhere in the book is that students be offered opportunities to take charge of their own learning and collaborate in course and instructional design decisions.

Opportunities for Co-Generation in Approaches to Instruction

As mentioned in Chapter 1, YA literature invites, encourages, and applauds student participation in the course design process. It reminds us that literacy and literature are sociocultural, and it encourages readers to be critically conscious community members. Each of the following sections features different ways you might engage students in classroom approaches that use YA literature in communities of practice. Although you may not be able to start the entire year or semester off with the approach described in Chapter 2, you can still find opportunities within existing course design structures that echo the theory. (Figure 3.2 is a road map outlining the instructional methods explored in the following sections.)

If at all possible, students must be encouraged to build their community and develop domains together. They must be given opportunities to consistently reflect on their community, and the approaches I outline here must work toward practice, or reification. (See Chapter 2 for more detail on the three concepts of domain, community, and practice.)

As a reminder, all of the pedagogical approaches described in this chapter do not necessarily reflect a revolutionary or liberatory commitment to equity, diversity, inclusion, and/or justice. But change often happens in increments (especially

Figure 3.2. Opportunities for co-generating curriculum using YA literature across instructional approaches.

- Read-Alouds
- Pairing/Bridging with Existing Course Texts
- Substitution
- Book Groups (Book Clubs or Literature Circles)
- Independent Reading
- Readers' Workshop

and frustratingly in schools, it seems), so I describe the ways in which we can begin to shift our practices using YA literature in a range of school systems: from the most traditionally rigid to examples in which teachers act as stewards, allowing their students to act with agency, significantly transform the curriculum, and center themselves in a community of practice (which is highlighted even more extensively in Chapter 4).

Instructional Approach 1: Read-Alouds, Co-Generated

For teachers in all settings, tightly structured or not, incorporating read-aloud practices into the classroom provides a meaningful and relatively simple way to infuse YA literature in the curriculum. In a more traditional vision of a read-aloud, the teacher selects a text and reads it aloud to students. Accompanying lessons and assessments vary significantly.

In a community of practice, the students need to be a part of the decision-making process: What domain are they interested in studying? Do they want to do a read-aloud at all? There are many options for shifting this practice to work in a more student-generated curricular space. In an American Literature course, for instance, the students would be the ones to develop the domain: What does it mean to be an American? One way to begin would be for students to explore and the teacher, as steward, to share several titles likely to appeal to students' interests related to their identified domain. If students are aware of any titles that might relate to the domain, they share these titles too.

Perhaps the students are interested in exploring the American Dream or studying immigration practices. They could discuss their interests related to the domain and identify titles they would like to hear in a read-aloud. At the start of class, often for just ten minutes or so, the book is read aloud while students listen actively. In that last sentence, you might note that I used the passive voice, and it was intentional. I encourage you to dig into the concept of a community of practice by having students rotate to each read a page aloud. You and the students might invite members of their community (within or outside of the school) or key stakeholders related to their domain of interest to read for ten minutes aloud at the start of class. In my own classroom, I found that secondary students of all ages clamored for the opportunity to sit as a group on the floor and simply take in the story. Some students don't enjoy reading aloud, and we honor other contributions they make to our community.

I start with read-alouds as an approach to instruction because most teachers can find space for ten minutes of reading each day. The aim of the read-aloud is to expose students to quality stories likely to engage them as adolescents rather than to pause frequently to hyper-analyze the text. The practice is similar to that advocated by former US Poet Laureate, Billy Collins, who, as part of his educational outreach efforts, launched a program that encourages school communities to read a poem a day. As Collins (n.d.) explains in his rationale for the project,

> Hearing a poem every day, especially well-written, contemporary poems that students do not have to analyze, might convince students that poetry can be an understandable, painless and even eye-opening part of their everyday experience. . . . Unless students really want to discuss the poem, there is no need to do so. The most important thing is that the poems be read and listened to without any academic requirements.

Sometimes we engage with read-alouds without any assessments, and instead the read-aloud inspires a student-designed unit of focus and the accompanying practice.

Read-alouds prove particularly beneficial for students who are emergent multilinguals, or those who need additional support in developing fluency, by giving them the opportunity to listen to the cadence of the language and develop receptive vocabulary. To expand student exposure to model readers representing multiple voices, you might also draw from audio recordings of titles selected by students and provide paper copies of the text to support students who need them.

A read-aloud is often used as a jumping-off point to engage in deep understanding about a topic. In the following vignette, Josh Thompson shares the transformative potential of read-alouds, taking the standard practice to a new level. Starting with a whole-class read-aloud of Jason Reynolds's (2017) *Long Way Down*, Josh built on his students' enthusiasm for the book by inviting them to work collaboratively with him to generate a student-centered, nontraditional unit that decentered him as the teacher in control and power. Josh describes how he took a step back and allowed his students to determine the design of the unit and the *practice.*

Redistributing Power in the Classroom with a Student-Centered Unit

Josh Thompson
Blacksburg High School, Blacksburg, VA
Twitter: @jthompedu

Step inside my classroom and you will quickly realize my passion for helping students (re)kindle a love of reading. I want to not only help students grow as readers but also empower them as individuals. Daily independent reading is, therefore, a staple in my classes. Students have choice in what they read, and I constantly expose them to a wide variety of great books in several ways, one of which is the read-aloud.

On one particular Friday in January 2019, I read aloud from the beginning of Jason Reynolds's *Long Way Down*, a book several students had asked about in the days prior. I chose an exciting moment in the book to stop, hoping to entice students into reading more on their own. And it worked, but much better than I had anticipated: students begged for more.

"Mr. Thompson, you *have* to keep going."

"Uh, I'm going to need you to keep reading."

"JT! You can't stop there!"

So I kept reading until the story arrived at an intense cliffhanger. The protests resurged, this time stronger. One student said, "I don't care what you had planned for today. We are finishing this book." Other students agreed, so I kept reading.

We finished the novel with ten minutes left in our ninety-minute class period. I asked my students to spend the remaining time responding to the book in whatever way they wished. I also requested that they tell me if they thought the read-aloud was a beneficial use of class time. The feedback was unanimously positive. Every student remarked that more teachers need to include books like *Long Way Down* in their classrooms.

The next day we talked about their reactions, and I mentioned the trend I noticed regarding the inclusion of the novel in curricula. Students asked, "Why don't more teachers read books like that in class?" Our conversation led to a discussion of the canon and which voices and experiences are included and excluded. Students were clearly engaged, asking insightful questions and discussing ideas with each other. Noticing their interest, I asked them if they thought we could work together to create resources for *Long Way Down*. If they believed so strongly that teachers should include the book in their curricula, then why not make a unit? At first they were skeptical, but once I explained what I thought it might look like and emphasized that it would be driven by their thoughts and ideas with my guidance and mentorship, the room buzzed with energy.

The process for our unit creation began with students brainstorming the types of documents, assignments, and activities they wanted in their unit. They utilized me as a resource, asking questions about my unit plans to better understand what goes into the work. Then we examined examples of materials I created for my teaching as well as assignment sheets and activities from their other classes. These documents served as mentor texts, not only allowing students to generate ideas but also guiding them as they created their own unit materials.

Once we had created a list of the items we wanted in our unit—prereading activities and projects, anticipatory sets, questions and assignments during and after reading, and formative and summative assessments—students chose the materials they wanted to make. They also had the option of working alone, in pairs, or in small groups, again a student-generated choice. We also wanted to make sure the workload was distributed equitably; therefore, each work assignment was discussed and voted on by the entire class.

The next several class periods ran as writers' workshops. Students researched, composed, and revised. During this time, I conferenced with each student or group, asking questions about their authorial choices and offering feedback. Some students even shared their materials with peers. Again, the classroom came alive.

After students had substantial drafts, as a class we reviewed everyone's work. I projected the materials on the smartboard, students thought to themselves about the quality of the work, and then they shared their feedback in a class-wide review. The author(s) of the work took notes. My students impressed me not only with their insightful comments but also with the questions they asked their reviewers. They cared about their work, both individual components and the collective unit, and their investment showed.

Following this review process, students returned to their materials, revised based on the feedback given, and submitted their final products. I also conferred with each student or group during this time. In the end, they created something they were proud of, so much so that they asked me to teach their unit in future classes.

While totally novel, this experience affirmed several beliefs I have about teaching, namely the necessity of student choice. It should center everything we do in our classrooms. My students had a say in every aspect of this unit creation, from the read-aloud that sparked it all to their final products. They knew I did a First Chapter Friday read-aloud every week, and they asked that *Long Way Down* be added to the list. If student agency didn't ground my teaching, I most likely wouldn't have continued the read-aloud—let alone decide to erase my plans and dive headfirst into this unit creation—and we all would have missed out on a transformative opportunity.

Moreover, I believe that the entire unit creation process operated as smoothly and effectively as it did because student ideas and decisions drove it. We planned class time together; their needs informed our design. Earlier, I noted how struck I was by the quality of their feedback and level of engagement during the review process. That didn't happen by chance. Students were invested in the work because *they* decided to do it. They *wanted* to do it, and they cared so much about it that they asked me to use their unit in the future. How many times have we as English language arts teachers lamented the lack of engagement and spark in student work during the writing process? How frequently do we create ways for our students to be invested in their writing opportunities? How often do we wish they wanted to share their work with others? This unit creation demonstrates the power of student choice.

But I want to lean into that emphasis on student agency and the tremendous impact it has on our classrooms. Yes, many of us incorporate student choice in various ways: we might let them decide what they want to read during daily independent reading, select the topic of their writing, choose the focus of their research, vote on the books to read during literature circles, among many other methods. However, how often do we set aside days or weeks and devote that time to something students want? Do we ever step aside and allow students to drive our classes and instruction? I know there are great teachers across the world who have done that work and continue to do it. I'm calling on more of us to join them. We have to be comfortable with the uncomfortable and unknown. To be truly transformative, student choice needs a redistribution of power in the classroom. Students need to be active agents in their learning; it's part of our obligations as teachers to honor that.

Furthermore, underscoring all of this project is the power of high-interest young adult literature. The book hooked them first. Without it, this moment wouldn't have happened.

Instructional Approach 2: Pairing/Bridging with Existing Course Texts, Co-Generated

Pairing, which is also called bridging, connects two or more texts with a common theme, topic, setting, character, narrative approach, etc. If you are expected to implement a classics-based curriculum, this approach allows for opportunity and space to introduce YA literature. Bridging is a concept that has been around for quite some time. In *From Hinton to Hamlet: Building Bridges between Young Adult Literature and the Classics*, Herz and Gallo (2005) model a vision of integration through bridging and literature circles. They encourage teachers to begin whole-class reading and study of a classic text with small-group reading and discussion of related young adult titles. Herz and Gallo offer specific recommendations for numerous classic novels that are commonly taught in American high school classrooms.

A concern with the pairing/bridging approach is that it continues to privilege canonical texts. In some school systems, the vast majority of curricular texts are canonical, with only one text, if any, attached or bridged to a recent young adult text. And in many cases, this isn't an even pairing, as the canonical text takes center stage in instruction; the YA text acts in an additive way. However, allowing a young adult text to take center stage or, at a minimum, be offered as an equal partner, can encourage thoughtful, deep discussions and provide great opportunities to critique the ways in which schools and curricula are structured. I offer this as a structure for teachers whose capacity to introduce young adult texts is limited, but it offers the least innovation and opportunity of all of the approaches discussed in this chapter.

Before you engage in the reading of a canonical text, I encourage you to read Borsheim-Black et al.'s (2014) article, "Critical Literature Pedagogy: Teaching Canonical Literature for Critical Literacy." Their framework offers dimensions of literary study that ask us not only to read *with* a text but also to read *against* a text. When we read *with* a text, we are participating in traditional reading classroom pedagogical practice, such as analyzing the story and literary devices, making connections, examining context, and identifying theme. But reading against the text draws from critical literacy and

> challenges students to consider not only what is written in the text but also what is not written that still accounts for the way the story works, the characters function, and how readers come to know and understand the world. Thus, reading against canonical literature means reading between the lines to expose and interrupt embedded, dominant narratives, power dynamics, and perceived normalcy espoused by and hidden in the text, including its inclusion in school curricula. (p. 125)

Using this framework with students to examine canonical literature, our community of practice might, for instance, utilize the chart from this article, which focuses on the dimensions of literacy instruction of canonicity, contexts, literary elements, and reader assessments, to drive discussions about their interests related to reading with and against texts. Having uncovered these interests, students should be able to develop a domain to study and then select a young adult text to use as a bridge to read against the canonical text. For instance, the students in our domain who are studying "What does it mean to be an American?" might take a required text like *The Grapes of Wrath*, focus on considering aspects like land use, and read with and against the text, and then pair/bridge a text like Angeline Boulley's (2021) *Firekeeper's Daughter* to study land rights. They might then use these texts to engage in conversations with key partners and advocate publicly for something like a local landback movement for Indigenous peoples. Students would identify topics of interest, and the teacher would act as steward and share titles of texts that would enhance discussion.

In the next two vignettes, two teachers who worked in the same school share how they paired texts in their classrooms as they worked with the required curricular text *To Kill a Mockingbird*. (Since the writing of these two vignettes, both teachers have moved to different school settings.) These teachers recognized that their students weren't connecting with *To Kill a Mockingbird*, which is a mainstay in US classrooms. Tiana's and Steven Ray's vignettes share some of the critique this popular, often required school text has received more generally in the last several decades. It is written through a white gaze (Morrison, 1998), particularly in terms of racism—perhaps to make it more palatable for white audiences. In a vignette later in this chapter, Morgan Jackson shares how Tom isn't a fully drawn character and how as a character he needs to die for Scout to learn about racism. Other critiques include the depiction of the Ewells. Grice et al. (2018) write,

> Mayella and her family would today represent the "white trash" or "redneck" stereotype of rural, working-class whites. This becomes problematic when the Ewells are the only narrative of rural, white, working-class characters that students are exposed to in literature. Tragically, they have become an archetype for the rural, white working class. (p. 19)

The Ewells are characterized in ways that are "emblematic of the racist, misogynistic attitudes that plagued the South during this time period" (p. 19), and these stereotypes are very real for students across the country. Beyond this, Atticus Finch is the white savior that the hegemonic system seeks.

Both of these teachers took their gut reactions to a required, canonical text and worked with their students to design a more student-centered approach. They imagined very different units, both of which used bridging for this text: Tiana paired *To Kill a Mockingbird* with *The Hate U Give* by Angie Thomas (2017), and Steven Ray paired the novel with *The Perks of Being a Wallflower* by Stephen Chbosky (1999). I have intentionally included the accounts of both of these teachers to demonstrate the possibilities when responding to student needs. Tiana's class chose to spend time examining authorship, focusing on the differences in the authors' voices and how these informed their texts, as well as analyzing the contexts of the two books and how they were different (and not so different) even though their settings are ninety years apart. Steven Ray's class chose to analyze trauma and explore in meaningful ways the treatment of youth by adult authors. His unit encouraged his students to write their own stories. My hope is that these different examples of pairing/bridging, both featuring the same required canonical text, demonstrate the potential of this instructional approach and reveal the ways in which teachers can decenter the classic and center the more relevant YA text. In both instances, the teachers stepped back from their positions of power to let their students drive the domains they themselves chose, demonstrating how they worked intentionally to build community. Tiana's students defined their domains by developing inquiry questions and leading Socratic seminars, and Steven Ray's students used interactive notebooks to make sense of the texts and develop their thinking.

Using Classical and Contemporary Texts to Empower Students to Think Independently

Tiana Song
Poudre Global Academy, Fort Collins, CO
Email: tsong@psdschools.org

The first year I taught high school, I was assigned to ninth-grade English. When I saw the required district reading list for ninth grade, I was excited to see the title *To Kill a Mockingbird.* I thought, "I think I remember really enjoying this novel?" As I prepared lessons for this text, I realized that I remembered very little about *To Kill a Mockingbird* (*TKaM*). This is an unpopular thing to say in my content area, but when I finished rereading *TKaM*, I felt disappointed and reluctant to teach it. When I told my colleagues that I felt the text was white-centered and didn't address the parallel racist realities many Black Americans face today, I got some unfriendly glares and comments. It was as though I had shouted the most inappropriate word about a classical text. Openly critiquing canonical texts can be tricky.

I want my students to learn how to think critically and to make decisions about their own learning. The ability to critique and think critically about why they believe what they believe is a necessary life skill. *TKaM* is a classic text, and many believe it deserves its place in the high school English curriculum, but I find it more valuable to leverage other contemporary texts to help students critique and understand the past concurrent with the present. In public high schools across the nation, the Black American perspective is told primarily by people who are not Black Americans—just as it is in *TKaM*. We cannot fully understand other perspectives until we hear the voices of the people who hold those perspectives (which is interesting because it's reminiscent of the commonly highlighted message of *TKaM* that we can't understand a man until we've walked a mile in his shoes). Thus, I made the decision not to use *TKaM* as the central text but rather as a highly critiqued supplemental text alongside the central YA text of *The Hate U Give*, which is told from the perspective of Black characters and was a text that students expressed interest in reading.

Below are highlights of the pedagogical process my students and I developed that paired the two texts side by side and encouraged students to explore similarities and differences and fostered independent thinking:

- Students developed inquiry questions to learn the historical context of both novels. This provided them with a better sense of the language, the characters, setting, themes, etc. *TKaM* is set in the 1930s and *The Hate U Give* is set in the present day. Students worked in groups during mini-lessons to share their questions and findings about the time periods and contexts. The goal of this activity was to create a foundational understanding of historical events that significantly impact each novel's characters. When discussing themes, topics, characters, or events from both novels, students had the contextual background knowledge to share and from which to generate their own connections and conclusions about how the past influences or affects the present.
- Reading specific excerpts from *TKaM* helped leverage conversation about how racial discrimination has evolved, as well as revealing flaws in the original text. Using excerpts while reading the entirety of *The Hate U Give* gave students the opportunity to critically examine both texts on current events and issues without having the students read the entire text. This centered the YA text and de-emphasized the canonical text.
- Racial discrimination was a central topic of discussion and was bound to other, smaller conversations students were interested in having, about issues such as redlining, slavery, segregation, police brutality, color blindness, and the list goes on. The students again as a class developed inquiry questions to decide what topics they wanted to research and discuss more deeply. Reading *The Hate U Give* encouraged discussions of these current issues around racism in America, such as police brutality, color blindness, and protesting.
- Socratic seminars and small-group discussions were essential to the process and entirely created and led by the students. Throughout the unit, students discussed the ways in which similar topics emerge in the excerpts from Harper Lee's novel and *The Hate U Give*. By giving students the opportunity to organize

and create questions centered on the ideas presented in the text and readings, they were able to use evidence to articulate their thinking. As students brought their own ideas and questions to the table, they often reflected on why they believe what they do, and they discovered how to support their thinking. When students have the ability to take charge of their own learning, they generate a classroom space that is productive, nonjudgmental, and welcoming to ideas.

- By pairing excerpts from an older text with the entirety of the new contemporary text, students created learning opportunities, making connections between past and current events. They discussed respectfully with their peers how their thinking grew and evolved, how they could critique two texts to better understand past and present issues, and how they felt empowered to draw their own conclusions by explaining in depth where their thinking came from.

The ability to teach with two texts can be enlightening and rewarding for both students and teacher. They can examine a topic, such as racial discrimination, but get two different voices, contexts, and experiences that allow them to make connections and think independently. It was all worth the uncertainty for me, because I know that when my students reflect on *To Kill a Mockingbird*, they will apply that novel's representation of racism to the realities of what is happening in our current culture. These students will remember *TKaM* and *The Hate U Give* as novels that taught them to critique works of art and to think critically and independently.

Pairing YA Literature with Problematic (and Increasingly Less-Engaging) Canonical Text Requirements

Steven Ray Parker
Wylie East High School, Wylie, TX
Email: steven.parker@wylieisd.net

Most adults in this country read Harper Lee's *To Kill a Mockingbird* at some point in their educational journey. I remember reading the novel almost thirty years ago in high school. I felt a strange kinship with Scout's vehement, foot-stomping beliefs around how the world should be. Growing up in the South, I could smell Miss Maudie's azaleas, feel the heat that drove children to play outside and forced adults to drink iced tea on porches, and empathize with Jem's tears at the courthouse due to the injustice that he perceives.

Lee's wit, sarcasm, and idyllic (albeit anachronistic) language has made this novel a ubiquitous staple on syllabi in most high schools. When I first started teaching this novel (a required ninth-grade text in my school district at the time), I knew I couldn't approach the instruction as my high school teacher did. *To Kill a Mockingbird* cannot be taught in isolation as a book study as it has in years past, focusing on character development, symbolism, foreshadowing, and so on. I thought I was on the cutting edge that first year when I introduced my students to New Historicism, allowing them an "in" to understand the book in context with its time. I also brought in "texture" texts that disrupted Lee's dreamlike language: videos of Black oppression, pictures and articles about the Great Depression, the exhaustive list of Jim Crow laws enacted in Alabama, Nina Simone's heartbreaking song "Strange Fruit." Although a handful of students walked this journey with me and enjoyed the book, I saw ennui in the eyes of most of them.

This was a failure. My postinstructional questioning focused on why the students didn't feel more connected to the novel even with the additional (and accessible) texture I introduced during the unit. The summer afterward, I began to flip that questioning back on myself. I crossed that line of reconsidering the canon itself. Was the novel accessible and accurate? Who was its intended audience? Why were we still teaching it?

A few years ago, I set two goals: first, I want to introduce readings in which all my students can see themselves, and, second, I want to introduce readings in particular that have positive representations of LGBTQIA+ persons. When I reviewed these goals, I had that moment all teachers have multiple times throughout the year: I have not only failed myself, but I have failed my students.

For me, growing up in the South made *To Kill a Mockingbird* "comprehensible"; growing up white made Scout's confusion "understandable"; growing up surrounded by deep-rooted systems of racism made the novel's plot "predictable." But the discrimination that is presented problematically in the book didn't equate to the discrimination I felt as a gay adolescent. My students wouldn't be able to relate to many—if any—of these components of the novel. Why would my students of color automatically empathize with Scout, Jem, and Dill simply because Mr. Robinson's fate was decided long before the trial? How was this novel any different from all of the other texts we offered? What would I have wanted to read when I was a student? Those were the questions that led me to seek another book to pair with *To Kill a Mockingbird*. The students and I worked together to identify a YA novel for pairing with the concepts they were passionate about. We worked to identify these concepts together. They sought an adolescent narrator who challenged the world's status quo. Ideally, this narrator would experience events in unreliable ways. Based on previous discussions, they also sought an example of positive representation of an LGBTQIA+ character. I mentioned that the *The Perks of Being a Wallflower* by Stephen

Chbosky (1999) might work well, and the students were interested in reading the book in order to make connections with *To Kill a Mockingbird*. From there, we asked ourselves how Charlie and Scout might exist in a universe that can be scrutinized through an academic lens.

I have to be forthright about my feelings and admit that I struggled at first. It was important to me that we weren't *comparing* Charlie's experience to Scout's—that we weren't privileging the classic text. As the students read, they elected to use interactive notebooks to "make sense" of what they were reading. Using the purest form of interactive notebooks, students took notes on the right side of the notebook. These notes stemmed from our classroom conversations and could be in many formats: bullets, sketchnotes, questions, word-for-word recitation, outlines, etc. (we review and practice all of these options at the beginning of the year). During the last few minutes of class, students furthered their understanding by reacting to what they had written via *interaction* on the left side of the notebook. The possibilities for this interaction are endless. Many students draw, some create foldouts, some repeat the words from the right side as found poetry on the left. Anything they choose to do is interacting with the text. Students who needed support created "word boxes" of the most important vocabulary they used in their notes. To align notes with the focus and reason for pairing these two texts, students questioned the narrators on the right side of their notebooks. We reminded ourselves every day that adults wrote these novels, yet the narrators are the students' age. We then asked ourselves, "What are the adult writers 'getting wrong' about the experiences of children?" Specifically, students were interested in thinking about the ways in which narrators unreliably recall events in their lives. We also had discussions about the implications of this in connection to trauma. Examples of questions they wrote include:

- Would Charlie remember only those (seemingly) positive interactions with his aunt? Wouldn't he feel discomfort throughout the novel?
- Are the friends in Charlie's group typical of teens? Are my friends like that?
- How can a six-year-old like Scout have that vocabulary? Should I know the words she uses?
- Why is Jem so protective of his little sister? Is that normal in most families?

Since their notes were already in question format on the right-hand side of the page, students internalized those questions and responded to them on the left side. It was typical to hear some giggling as they answered their own questions. I often heard comments akin to, "My brother doesn't do that!" or "Charlie's friends sound like they're teachers!" Through this process, students designed their own path as they considered how adult writers writing as adolescent or child narrators aren't always accurate in their portrayals of youth. I wanted to give them agency to guide the class with the questions they were most curious about and also allow them to question the "importance" of a novel that has been historically praised. Very few felt any kinship with the children in the required *To Kill a Mockingbird* other than "the treatment of Tom Robinson is wrong." They also found Atticus's distant emotional relationship with his children in direct opposition to how he is portrayed as the hero of the novel. However, many found a character they identified with in *The Perks of Being a Wallflower*. High school students are quite familiar with unrequited love, the desire to be accepted, and the questioning of one's identity. In one form or another, most can speak to trauma they have experienced in their own lives, and they made these connections in class and in their notebooks.

The mere notion that they could question a writer (or even me and my position) was a hurdle that several students struggled to overcome. I wanted to decenter myself, so I often told them, "I don't care what your opinion is, I just want you to have an opinion!" I remember one particular student's comment from that first week. I noticed that Neola (pseudonym) had stopped writing questions in her notebook. I asked her after class about this uncharacteristic move. Neola looked me in the eyes and said, "I think we are breaking the rules. I don't know how to say that a writer is wrong." She needed encouragement to *break* with reading instruction from her past concerning author's purpose, theme, locating figurative language, and—well, we all know the staples of teaching a text that will test well on standardized exams. I knew about Neola's own experience with discrimination as a Native American girl and past trauma, and I didn't want to give her a directive. Neola was reticent about questioning someone as "wise" as Atticus or as "thoughtful" as Scout or as "confused" as Charlie. Thinking about her quandary, I replied, "Neola, if I were to write about what it is like to be *you*, what would I get wrong because I'm a man and I'm white?" She paused, looked down at my desk, and smiled. "I get it," she replied. And isn't that the comment we all want to hear as educators as we try to move out of the way of students as they find their voice in the classroom? *I get it.*

Bridging allows students to analyze and critique the historicity of texts in classrooms, but canonical texts will not be represented frequently in most communities of practice units. If our goal is to work toward genuine communities of practice in our classrooms, canonical texts will most likely be decentralized as students increasingly select texts that meet the needs of their identified domains. Teachers seeking to rattle the cage will consciously try to disrupt rigidity in traditional text instruction in more substantive ways that invite students to determine how they want to analyze texts and what they seek to explore as a community.

Ideally, teachers won't feel tied to classic texts, and students can help select texts that align with their identified domains. But in some schools, like the one Tiana and Steven Ray used to work in, classic texts are required, so bridging afforded them opportunities to center YA literature relevant to student interests. Steven Ray's and Tiana's vignettes demonstrate a strong desire to offer relevant texts that elevate young people. After several iterations of teaching *To Kill a Mockingbird*, Tiana managed to offer a more balanced set of texts to avoid the "undue focus on the victimization of Black bodies" that Morgan Jackson discusses in a vignette later in the chapter.

Educators disagree widely about how canonical texts should be used, and I'd argue that we should find the right texts that fit our students' identified domains, and students should be involved in the decision-making process. Canonical texts can be leveraged in powerful ways to critique structures and systemic barriers to equity. Their inclusion reminds us about what we value in schools, and Tiana and Steven Ray chose to approach the challenges they were experiencing by including portions of the classic text to offer room for students to critique the system and to create space and structures that honored the voices of the young people in their care. Both teachers used the canonical text as an opportunity and invitation for students to critique the ways in which we structure and value the literature we include in our classrooms.

It's also important to find ways for students not just to participate in class but also to engage in reification, or practice. Ideally, this reification is connected to their school, local, and global communities and reaches outward to make a concrete change.

Instructional Approach 3: Substitution, Co-Generated

A discussion about bridging is likely leading to the question: How might we *replace* the classic texts required in our curricula? When we as English teachers ask adults to share the titles they read in their high school English courses, most often they will first list the classics they loathed before addressing titles they loved and appreciated (if there were any). As teachers of English language arts, we have a shared understanding that many, if not most, people don't report positive experiences related to their high school English classrooms and/or the texts they read in these classrooms.

We teach what we know. Examining what we know, how we learned in school, and how we can expand these understandings is critical for us as educators. Those who defend and teach only the canon are (intentionally or not) teaching racialized lessons and signaling whose stories they believe matter (Haddix & Price-Dennis, 2013, Borsheim-Black & Sarigianides, 2019). Those in power (victors, colonizers) have not only determined what our history books say is important to know, but they have also seemingly determined on a longish list of "classic" texts that belong in schools. Classic texts included in the standard English curriculum are often limited to those eighteenth- and nineteenth-century British and American authors who promoted the culture in power at the time: white, cisgender, heterosexual, male, Christian.

If you pick a few random schools in the United States and pull their curricula, you'd likely find a similarity across their required texts. (Although there is some variety. After working in schools for many years, I'm still unclear about precisely *which* books are actually in the "canon" because every time I think I've figured it out, a teacher tells me their school can't possibly send students to college without [text], and they name a text I have never seen on other lists.) Gay (2000) writes about the "constraining manacles of mainstream canons of knowledge and ways of knowing" (p. 35). Your school is one place where freedom from these manacles can begin, if it hasn't already. I'm not arguing that we must shoot the canon out of a cannon, but unless students, in a community of practice, determine that a text matches their domain—their passions, the big questions they have about the world—we need to recenter. *Their* concerns should be prioritized over a canonical text that we or our school district personally values.

It must be stated again: the vast majority of the students in English classrooms *don't actually read the assigned books.* In a disheartening survey by Ivey and Broaddus (2001) that still applies to classrooms today, students ranked their classrooms as one of the least likely places to find reading materials. In Wilkinson et al.'s more recent 2020 study, adolescents more often described their own intrinsic reasons for reading—reading to learn, reading to relax, reading that allows them to absorb or escape, reading that develops empathy, reading that offers social capital, and reading for excitement. This study's findings led the authors to encourage teachers to allow students more time to read for pleasure and during class time. This seems to suggest that extrinsic factors like grades are less motivating than a pure love of reading—something that can be fostered with careful consideration of course design and instructional approaches, along with a large bookshelf of high-interest and high-quality texts. We are inadvertently committing what Gallagher (2009) describes as "readicide," or the "systematic killing of the love of reading, often exacerbated by the inane, mind-numbing practices found in schools" (p. 2).

Even if it feels as if our curriculum is under lock and key, it's important to ask *why* a text is required. The substitution process might begin with a determination of the motivations for teaching a particular text already in the curriculum. Perhaps a unit topic is highly valued in the department. A teacher might ask students to work as a community of practice to develop a set of interests related to that required topic. They can then form their own domain, which is connected to the required course topic, substitute the classic with a YA text that engages the community in issues relevant to their domain. The aim is to have the students, as a community of practice, build a domain. If the required curriculum has a checklist of items you must cover, give that checklist to students and invite them to design the course curriculum as they rattle their district's scripted or rigid curricular cage that privileges a classic. When students select the title, they will be more likely to read it—because they selected it.

As an example of what this might look like using an actual text, we might ask ourselves why *The Scarlet Letter* is often considered essential reading for tenth graders. Is the text used to enhance study of a particular theme (a discussion of isolation, for example) or time period or literary era (Puritan America or American Romanticism)? If the goals underpinning the inclusion of the title in the curriculum are not readily evident, it might be a good opportunity for students to consider an alternative, and teachers might need to step in, depending on the district, to pitch this justification to key stakeholders (gatekeepers, *cage*keepers). If these goals are identified as necessary elements of the course, students, as a community of practice, can select and write a justification for a young adult text that meets the same goals and *also aligns with an identified domain*. For instance, if the goal for using *The Scarlet Letter* is to discuss the theme of isolation, students might identify a domain related to themes of isolation but might use Eric Gansworth's (2020) *Apple: Skin to the Core* to think deeply about this theme, along with other, related themes of interest, like community. The related themes might evolve through discussion, and students might then delve deeply into other topics, like settler colonialism. They might then read Nikki Grimes's (2019) *Ordinary Hazards* and discuss these same concepts of isolation and community, closely considering the themes as they are presented across literature.

The community of practice defines the domain, checks in regularly on their community, and determines how their learning evolves as they explore their domain and the texts they have selected. They have rich discussions about what practice (or assessment) might emerge from their learning. As discussed in Chapter 2, this practice will, ideally, be outward-facing and relevant to their school, local, and global communities. Perhaps students might each go into their community to interrogate the ways in which isolation appears locally and work to build stronger, more communal structures. It's important to note that the community of practice created around this unit should not stop there. It offers a beginning step toward ways we can rattle the cage, but the aim is to work toward designing the whole curriculum with students, rather than simply substituting one single text in a yearlong, traditional curricular approach. In my metaphor, this is still upholding the bars of the cage, but it is slowly filling the cage with new ideas until its walls pry apart and ultimately fall down.

Instructional Approach 4: Book Groups (Book Clubs or Literature Circles), Co-Generated

Our own positionalities determine our lists of the texts we value and elevate in our classrooms. Rather than uplifting specific texts and requiring the same texts of all students, intentionally asking students to select and read different books across our lists has stronger potential to make our students more valuable contributors to an even more "educated" pluralistic society. We don't want our students to share the exact same life experiences, so we should also want them to have a diversity of reading experiences to invite more viewpoints and perspectives to the table.

Think about how this might look in a classroom space: Perhaps students were intrigued by public discussions in their community about critical race theory. For their domain, they are interested in looking at this theory and the ways we structure systems in America and deeply diving into this topic that is so controversial and so widely misunderstood across our nation. (Of note: This is just the tip of the iceberg of the complexity of critical race theory, but it allows an entry point for students to engage in public discussions about the topic.) Students might just take a small nugget of this theory and identify various systems they are each interested in analyzing, which might naturally lead to book groups. One group might use a book like Ibi Zoboi's (2017) *American Street* to think about immigration; this book offers students opportunities to discuss the American Dream, where for one character, freedom comes at a cost. Another group might be interested in examining how our country has historically and currently expressed hatred within its policies, systems, and practices and thus might select Traci Chee's (2020) *We Are Not Free* as one of their texts to read and discuss. Or a group of students might be interested in examining structural marginalization, class, and transphobia in our country and might use Kacen Callender's (2020) *Felix Ever After* to center their discussions. Or a group of students might be interested in examining Indigeneity, tribal sovereignty, tradition, and resilience and might use Cynthia Leitich Smith's edited (2021) *Ancestor Approved: Intertribal Stories for Kids*. Students can determine what they are interested in learning about, and these decisions drive their text selection. In these examples, students can have contemporary conversations within encouraging spaces that allow them to think critically about space and place.

In a true community of practice, students will select books from endless possibilities, rather than from a teacher-determined list. You might collect and fund small numbers of shared texts across several years to keep these titles current and then acquire new titles each year based on student interest. In the best scenario, students will identify titles of interest, and you can then acquire funding (recommendations in Chapter 4) for these new titles. Based on student preferences, you can group students, typically three to five students for each title. You can certainly employ intentional grouping strategies that provide necessary support for particular learners while still honoring student interest. In my classroom, for example, students first develop domains of interest. Then we think about texts that would help us discuss these domains and help us engage in our local and/or global community with our practice. Following these conversations, they identify their top three domain and text choices; we attempt to honor first choices whenever possible.

During the first book group meeting, you might ask students to determine a reading schedule based on the days they will meet and a novel completion date you have co-determined. I find that allowing students to select their own reading schedules helps them take ownership of the reading deadlines. If groups will meet four times before they should finish the books, for example, group members might plan to read a quarter of the book in preparation for each group meeting. In the meetings that follow, usually twenty to forty minutes long, students engage in conversation around the pages they have read for that session. I aim to provide a few days between group meeting dates to accommodate student out-of-school schedules and allow time for reading and group preparation.

Teachers using traditional book clubs often draw from Daniels's (2002) literature circle model and ask students to practice participating in certain roles that ultimately guide the conversation. One student, for example, serves as a "discussion director" and, in preparation for the group meeting, generates questions to pose to the group. Another student might volunteer to serve as a "literary luminary" and cite thoughtful and thought-provoking passages from the text to discuss with group members. And another student might don the role of "illustrator" and create an artistic representation of some element of the text. Daniels encourages students to select new roles for each group meeting so they can gain varied skill practice and contribute in various ways to their group discussions.

These roles can be limiting, however, so I ask students to define their own roles, which extend beyond those advocated by Daniels. This allows them to consider how they can use their strengths to contribute to our community of practice. Ideally, students will develop skills to participate in conversations about books without having to depend on and prepare to assume a single role; they will draw from a wide repertoire of skills as necessary in an authentic discussion of books, and they will do so in roles connected to their interests. To that end, when we do choose to start with roles, we gradually eliminate them after a few meetings in order to foster students' independent engagement with the texts and their groups. With students who have worked with book groups and demonstrated their ability to talk freely about books for sustained periods of time, I don't use literature circle roles at all.

In the following vignette, Kellee Moye shares how she uses in-class book clubs to build a classroom community through student-centered approaches. Unlike with literature circles, the students in her in-class book clubs share the same job, and the students' inquiry rather than the teacher's questions drive the approach. She finds that this approach helps her middle school students develop stamina for reading and allows them to share their love for books.

In-Class Book Clubs: Building Community, Stamina, and Reading Love

Kellee Moye
Hunter's Creek Middle School, Orlando, FL
Twitter: @kelleemoye, @unleashreaders
Facebook: Unleashing Readers

In-class book clubs are one of my favorite units, and my students say the same. They are my version of literature circles but with one change: my students' only job is to read, analyze, and discuss. These book clubs build community, stamina, and reading love in my classroom. Book clubs are successful because of the same factors that Harvey Daniels (2002) cites for literature circles: engagement, choice, responsibility, and research. Unlike his literature circles, however, my students all have the same "job," and my questions and opinions don't drive instruction. Instead, students generate their own ideas, insights, and inquiries (Brabham & Villaume, 2000).

As a teacher, I am always working to grow professionally to give my students the best possible instruction in the classroom, but one practice that has been a common theme throughout all of my years with a literacy class is a version of a book club. Although the way I implement them has drastically changed over the years as I've learned and grown from scholarship, approaches I've gathered from conferences, and insights from students, the main elements have stayed the same: students *choose* their texts, *collaborate* to discuss the texts, and *collect* thoughts about the texts. Also, each year students love book clubs and share how they grow in their reading skills, critical thinking abilities, and love of reading, and to me, this matters the most.

Currently, my implementation begins when I ask students to share topics they are interested in thinking about. From this list, I pull any book related to these topics for which

I've been able to get a small set of texts funded, and the students participate in a book pass of all the books I can garner. Then I have students list their top three texts on an index card with their names. This process is completely silent because I really want students to pick the book they want to read and not what their friends want to read. I know their interest in topics might change when they see the texts too. I then arrange the index cards into groups of three to five depending on what books were chosen. The next day the students sit in their book clubs and determine their reading schedules. I give them the overall time period and ask them to come up with a schedule of pages to read by each book club meeting. Most groups come up with a daily reading goal too, but this is optional.

We create class norms for what they want their book club meetings to look like. I then provide reading time every day—and I read along with students to demonstrate the value I place on the act of reading. We also do other class activities that they help co-determine, except on book club meeting day, which is held on Mondays because I want the students to have the weekend to read before our meetings.

One thing I didn't like about traditional literature circles was the unevenness of "jobs" and that only one student was responsible for the ongoing conversation during meetings. It didn't feel like they were building community. Because of my discomfort with that approach, all of my students have the same task while reading: come up with five open-ended discussion questions or topics they want to talk about during the meeting. We work together to brainstorm thought-provoking questions. We co-generate generic questions that will work with any book to support my middle schoolers in this process, and they develop questions they might discuss about topics in the books they are interested in learning more about. As students read, they also create and add to a word wall, so I ask them to write down any words they don't know and figure out what those words mean. Students then share the words and meanings in their groups and discuss them before putting them on our word wall.

Recently I have added a nonfiction component. At the 2018 NCTE Annual Convention, I went to one of Kelly Gallagher's sessions, and he shared a way he connects nonfiction and fiction when his students are reading novels: he has the students find nonfiction text features that connect to their novels. I decided to try this with my students, and we all loved it! As a book club, my students explored topics related to the books and identified two nonfiction elements (maps, graphs, images, etc.) that would enhance readers' knowledge of the topic they are studying. They then identified on what page they would place the element and explained why it was important.

Finally, at the end of the unit, I ask students to examine the standards my school expects students to achieve and to select a few standards to explore in their group. They write about their topics and texts independently to demonstrate their progress, which allows me to assess their learning and connect it to the standards. The groups then decide on action projects to speak out about their texts and connect with more public audiences.

I have found that the student autonomy and choice built into in-class book clubs allow for stronger engagement in the learning process than other novel-centered in-class activities. Most students end in-class book clubs with a positive outlook on the experience and a higher regard for reading overall.

Student-centered book clubs give students the freedom to discuss topics of interest and titles they choose, which creates positive reading experiences. Using book clubs offers my students choice, and it leads to an independence in their learning and an encouragement to continue to learn on their own. I trust in them, and in turn, they develop strong collaborative skills and are liberated from traditional classroom structures.

As Kellee's instructional approach demonstrates, students can determine what domain they wish to study, can develop their community as they read, and can develop action projects (their practice) based on their interests. Kellee is able to rattle the cage while still operating within the realities of her school: she has to consider which books she can get funded in small class sets, and she needs students to work together to complete standards-based assessments related to their texts.

When students are exploring what their practice might be related to their topic and book group texts, they might consider documents, projects, and writing that will allow them not only to think about their community but also to act as a part of and within that community. In one of my classes, the students all read books about the same topic, and they fashioned a quilt, with each square representing ideas from their texts, to hang in a public space. Again, the goal here is to foster a classroom community in which reading is valued and students see themselves as important participants in the larger community; their recommendations and participation matters, and their involvement in their community is valued. They are positioned as important contributors of knowledge related to the domains they choose to study.

Instructional Approach 5: Independent Reading, Co-Generated

Engaging in book clubs and read-aloud practices, substituting one text for another, and bridging texts in the classroom certainly create worthwhile opportunities to use YA literature in the classroom. Each of these practices can be conducted within a critical framework that requires student and community collaboration and voice. To expand on these approaches and allow for more active individual student choice in the selection of titles, you might also create and implement independent reading practices. Students participating in such practices read both inside and outside of school, a particularly viable option in settings where curricular guidelines are strict and leave little time for extras during the available class time.

This approach to independent reading centers on the belief that students, when allowed to self-select domains and texts, are more likely to engage in reading and, in the process, develop both skills and dispositions that foster their ability and willingness to read more. The implementation of an independent reading program involves several elements, including student choice, time for community building, and creative opportunities for responses to texts. I allow students to select any topic they wish to study and any text they wish to read—from novels to poetry to graphic novels to nonfiction to short story collections to drama. In my class, they are free to read anything. Students borrow titles from my classroom or the school library or bring in texts they have acquired elsewhere.

One co-generated approach to independent reading is to allow all students, as a community of practice, to select a domain they wish to study together, and then students select independent texts that will provide a stronger understanding of this domain. A second co-generated approach is to allow students to select individual domains of study and then group students with similar domains to discuss what they are learning. Regardless of the approach, to start, you might allow students fifteen to twenty-five minutes for reading during each class meeting, typically at the start or end of the period. I've found that twenty minutes allows students to genuinely engage in their texts. If students look disengaged, I invite them to check out the bookshelf to find a new text. If they aren't enjoying a text, I encourage them to put it down and try another text, avoiding a reading rut. During this time, I conference with individual students about how they are thinking about their domain and their reading, record assessment information that allows me to determine progress and areas for further instruction, and model the reading process by sitting down with a book myself. Whenever time allows, I encourage students to engage in book raves and share a teaser about a book they are enjoying and would recommend to their peers. Providing opportunities to read and talk titles during class results in a great pedagogical reward—namely, the creation of a community in which reading is a shared, validated, enjoyable activity.

Because students are reading various titles over a period of time, we must think creatively about assessment, or what I've been referring to as the *practice* part of a community of practice. Sometimes students will want to work in groups of related domains to develop their practice together. One year, I had three students who were interested in LGBTQ+ topics, and together they developed a podcast. The episodes differed because their interests and books differed, but their podcast offered layers of topics that shared a domain. Another year, the students developed the domain "Why we read." They were most interested in reading a diverse set of texts that followed many different topics, and this was one way they centered their classroom conversations. They designed practices that allowed them to participate in their school and local communities to share publicly what they had learned and to engage in conversations with community leaders. Similar domains offer teachers more flexibility in determining what the practice looks like.

Although various means of assessment would be appropriate and effective for specific domains, students might center their practice on assessment options that are formative (e.g., one-pagers, which I describe in the next chapter) and summative (e.g., reading portfolios and culminating, outward-facing choice projects). In alignment with the choice nature of the independent reading program, I invite students to select how they will respond to their independent reading titles within each of these assessments. I encourage students, over the duration of each semester, to respond creatively to four of the texts they chose to read in order to develop a portfolio to be shared at our book fair. Although some students will read fifteen titles or more in this span, others need this amount of time to complete four, so this approach encourages students to dig into four titles more deeply and doesn't generate more work for students who read more. I also engage students in regular reading conferences to discuss their reading and their overall progress. Upon identifying areas for further support, I provide both individual support and, for those areas of need identified across the class, group and whole-class lessons focused on reading strategies. In Chapter 4, I explain in detail the formative and summative assessments I use for independent reading, along with strategies and structures for supportive reading conferences.

In the following vignette, Jennifer Walsh shares how independent reading can lead into a larger unit of study. Her students chose independent YA texts related to social justice topics of interest. Each student studied their text and social justice topic and then completed a multigenre project. They then read a shared classroom text. During this shared reading, students were able to use their knowledge from their independent texts and social justice topics to strengthen the overall classroom conversations about social justice issues. Their summative assessment was a synthesis essay that allowed students not only to synthesize their independent social justice topic and YA text with the shared text, but also consider and present actionable steps they could take toward social justice.

Exploring Social Injustice through Independent Choice, Historical Context, and Synthesis

Jennifer L. Walsh
Forsythe Middle School, Ann Arbor, MI
Instagram: @readergirl
Twitter: jhank623

A few years ago, after the events in Charlottesville, Virginia, where a woman was killed during a KKK rally, I realized that I had to do something more to bring home the issue of social justice to my eighth-grade language arts classes. I was especially rattled by the anti-Semitic language being chanted throughout this event. It seemed as though our country was taking a step backward instead of forward. Because I live in an incredibly liberal town, my efforts received a lot of applause. I realize that may not be the case for others, but I believe social justice is a vital issue for us to teach, regardless of the context in which we teach. Below I describe the unit I created and adapt and teach today.

Phase One: Selecting Independent Social Justice Topics for Independent Reading and a Mini-Multigenre Project

Students independently read young adult novels that include issues of contemporary social injustice. I share as many books as I'm aware of that relate to the topics and do many book talks to introduce the students to texts. One day I even ran down to the school book fair during class to purchase all of their remaining copies of Jason Reynolds and Brendan Kiely's (2015) *All American Boys* because it was relevant to our conversation about current events, and I wanted students to be able to read it.

Based on student interests that semester, I ultimately decided to pivot, and we spent the entire second semester of school and our classwork threading together the various units under a social justice umbrella to align with student interests. We began by defining what social justice is and what it means to different people. Students wrote about the definitions and then we launched into our own research. Students co-generated a list of contemporary social justice issues to jump-start their thinking. Their writing led them to choosing a topic to explore in more depth, and they shared their topics with others in the community who had additional insights. This launched our mini-multigenre unit in which students were able to research their topics, learn new knowledge, take notes, create two products in different genres they felt expressed the heart of their topic, and present it to the class. This ended phase one of our social justice umbrella unit.

Phase Two: Reading a Shared Whole-Class Novel

Next, we incorporated a recent young adult novel of their choosing to talk about historical social justice issues. Throughout this unit, students wrote about the social injustices the characters experienced as well as what this kind of social injustice looks like today. They agreed that we had not reached a point of equity in the United States of America.

We discussed social justice throughout moments in history, such as slavery in 1776 New York and the Holocaust. Students don't get this far in their American History course (hello, Reconstruction, apparently that's all we have time for). As Laurie Halse Anderson wrote in *Speak*, "Every year they say we're going to get right up to the present, but we always get stuck in the Industrial Revolution. We got to World War I in seventh grade—who knew there had been a war with the whole world?" (p. 7). We discussed historical background and contexts and found and watched videos from different time periods, and then students wrote about why we choose to treat other humans so poorly. This is one of those questions my students were exploring the entire semester, and it kept coming up as a topic of interest. We also wrote about what it means to listen to a leader who doesn't have everyone's best interests at heart and wants to scapegoat a certain group of citizens. Many asked how people in Germany could have gone along with what Hitler was proposing, so we also examined motivations and what it means to look for a leader to pull a nation out of a "slump." We did a lot of article reading, and students wrote in their notebooks about these topics as well.

Phase Three: Writing a Synthesis Essay

Our social justice unit ended with a synthesis essay that brought together the different areas students had learned about related to social injustice (historical contexts and the personal topic they selected through their independent reading and research). In the essay, they outlined social injustices in each of these different individual units, and they surmised why people might treat others in the ways they did. Why does one group of people feel superior over others? How much does fear enter into this equation? What would make one group of people feel they can just rip groups from their land and/or force labor on other groups of people? This last is a practice chronicled for centuries. What does modern-day slavery look like? How can you take action to help with these issues? What actions can you take to make this world a better place and work toward an end to social injustices? All of the writing students had done over the course of the semester in each of these individual units was co-designed to help them formulate their thoughts and use the evidence they had gathered. By far, this was the most impact a school semester has had on my twenty-nine years of teaching. By weaving all of these individual units together to help eighth graders (and me) explore humanity and consider how they can actionably improve it, we think about how we can become compassionate thinkers, humanitarians, and (hopefully) politicians.

Jennifer's unit emerged from student interests, and their domain evolved as they considered deeply the topics that mattered to them. They were engaged with contemporary topics they saw in the news and felt emotions about political leadership. As Jennifer's unit demonstrates, she was a steward of knowledge, and her eighth graders drove the instruction. Ideally, units such as these are steps toward action, and students develop practice that allows them to engage with their community. As Jennifer notes, her students developed as a community as they shared insights. If she had chosen to take this community activity further, she could have leveraged the collective knowledge gleaned from the synthesis essays to consider other ways the students might engage with their community. This unit focused on a student-driven domain and demonstrates how the interests of a community can evolve and how instruction can adapt to community needs.

Instructional Approach 6: Readers' Workshop, Co-Generated

I close with readers' workshop as an instructional approach because it can be leveraged to open up possibilities for incorporating many of the instructional approaches raised in this chapter. Readers can move in and out of independent reading, book groups, and shared whole-class texts within this model and do so flexibly to deepen their thinking about their domain, community, and practice. Thus, it can serve as an umbrella over many of the other instructional approaches described in the chapter.

The readers' workshop model is essentially a student-centered and student-driven course design model—or it *should* be. Education companies and publishers have capitalized on this model and developed prepackaged programs from this model. I'm wary of these programs because they're designed without knowing anything about the most important influencing factors on your course design—your students and your community. The purpose of readers' workshop is to build or sustain a community of readers that is engaged and both individualized and *collaborative*. The infinite number of topics of study and the hundreds of thousands of YA texts available make readers' workshop even more relevant and engaging for students. I urge you to work with students to design and co-generate a workshop program that fits with student and community needs and interests rather than purchasing any kind of prepackaged curriculum. For instance, perhaps a public read-aloud would become a beloved part of the community, or maybe local authors would be interested in participating in the process, or perhaps an existing event has the potential to connect students more powerfully with those around them. These kinds of activities—generated by and with your students—offer more potential than handing out perforated worksheets that are disconnected from your community and context. Within this section, I highlight two different approaches to the process of creating readers' workshop (my own and that of a literacy curriculum facilitator), each of which offers options that can be adapted to the needs and interests of your students and community.

The workshop model, which was popularized with Atwell's (1998) *In the Middle: New Understandings about Writing, Reading, and Learning*, is grounded in the idea that students should be treated like adult readers, able to self-select, put down, and discuss with peers and adults the titles they read. This aligns with the potential of independent reading, but it offers a more significant collaborative aspect in its design. During class time, students read silently, meet with peers and the teacher to talk quietly about their reading and/or engage in written conversation, participate in book groups or pairs, and set and assess their individual reading goals. You might decide with students, for instance, to utilize this method one day each week, or you might structure your entire curriculum around this model.

The workshop approach encourages teachers to attend to logistical details to ensure smooth implementation. Your physical classroom would likely include access to a variety of young adult texts, typically through the creation and maintenance of a strong classroom library filled with new and relevant titles, as well as comfortable and cozy spaces in which to read them. You might also want to create a conversation corner where students can talk quietly with their peers without distracting others who are reading in the room. As independent reading time evolves, students will have read more books, and they will be able to recommend titles to each other. Given the choice element inherent in this model (and with all independent reading), it's also helpful if *you* carve out time to read the books you include in the classroom library. This ensures that you also have knowledge when recommending texts to students.

Formative assessments include working with students to discuss their progress in order to understand their growth, but also to encourage them to consider how their knowledge has evolved related to their domain. Regular check-ins with the community of practice allow students to recommend articles and texts to one another as they progress. If they are working on a shared group domain, they should be provided time to check in about progress related to their knowledge development. During this time, students might suggest opportunities for practice so they can share their knowledge with others. In addition to using conferencing methods advocated in the previous section and in the next chapter, one way I assess student progress is by asking students to maintain dialogue journals through which they engage in written conversation with their peers and with me.

In the example I discuss here, however, I share how readers' workshop can work when students are studying different, individual domains. Over the course of every other week, I ask students to write a dialogue journal with another student member in the community of practice. At the start of readers' workshop, we co-generate questions that will help students define their domains, or topics they are interested in studying and learning more about. Sometimes these are issues they are passionate about, like climate change, and other times they know of a book they are interested in reading, and they develop a domain related to that text. For instance, a student might know they want to read *Grown* by Tiffany D. Jackson (2020), and they might define their domain of interest as human trafficking.

We co-generate questions each week for response in their dialogue journals, but I also encourage students to take these conversations in whatever direction they want and need to go. One co-generated prompt that we developed to start the activity was:

- ▲ What are you interested in studying—what is your domain? Are there others in the class who share similar domains?

Students then share out what they wrote about, and we write all of the domains on the board and match students with shared interests to become dialogue journal partners. Each week the students write and respond to the entries, validating knowledge and literary insights, sharing perspectives, and posing questions for further conversation. As domains evolve or shift, we have occasionally switched writing partners to allow new students to work together. In these notebooks, students doodle, take notes on mini-lessons instructed by their peers and me, brainstorm ideas, jot down topics they'd like to explore and books they've finished or want to read, and so forth. The dialogue journals act as a written conversation, a collection of their thoughts about shared domains, and as inspiration for their reader thoughts and progress. Students write back and forth to each other and with me to explore other questions that we co-generate, such as:

- ▲ What kinds of books are you reading to help you grow your knowledge? What types of books do you like to read? In what ways might you stretch or challenge yourself as a reader and thinker?
- ▲ What are your strengths as a reader and thinker, and how do you plan to improve?

Students explore and learn more about their domains while working in community with one another, working specifically with their dialogue partners to grow their knowledge. Each student is working on an independent domain, but because they are paired intentionally, they are able to share resources and thinking and grow together. As they learn more, we begin to think about how they might develop a form of practice as a way to share their learning. One example of a co-generated question we developed for dialogue journal responses was:

- ▲ How might you work with others in our community to develop a form of practice that shares your new knowledge and would be important to our local community or the world?

I find the dialogue journals to be particularly useful in determining student knowledge, strengths, and areas of growth; this informs the content of the group and the individual support I provide as well as the mini-lessons designed for whole-class participation.

Readers' workshop sessions generally begin with mini-lessons, but I never preset my mini-lessons before I meet and work with my students; instead, these lessons always grow from student needs and interests. Sometimes the needs are related to the domains students are studying, and other times the needs are focused on ways they can strengthen their reading and/or writing. Typically, my students work independently with their dialogue partners, but they might also choose to work in a group with a shared domain of interest and dialogue about their domain together. These groups can be dynamic and may fluctuate as student interests fluctuate. The mini-lessons can be related to domains and be group-focused or they can address the whole class. I always try to involve students in the planning of a mini-lesson. We have open discussions about their knowledge gaps and needs as readers. We keep a working list of current knowledge and aspects of their domains they want to learn more about and the support they are seeking. They write these topics on the wall of the classroom. Then students claim a topic they are interested in teaching to their peers, and I work with students independently to design ten- to fifteen-minute lessons for their classmates. Some of the mini-lessons students and I have instructed have included the following:

- Finding articles to support our group-identified domains
- Setting and working toward goals
- Rereading strategies
- Learning about different genres and forms of writing

As an example of a mini-lesson, one student designed a lesson in which he discussed how we could and should push traditional conceptions of genres and genre sorting (shelving books according to their genres, such as sci-fi or nonfiction). He invited his peers to analyze a text that could fall into at least three genres and asked them to think about the benefits and consequences of genre sorting and how this practice impacts the reading community and the ideas in text. Another student asked peers to think about peritext, the materials offered by authors, editors, publishers, and printers that surround the main text of books, such as cover illustrations, author bios, back cover promo copy, etc. Students analyzed their current independent YA novels and shared the ways the peritext influenced their thinking and reading. (On an interesting tangent, students can also examine the epitext of the book, or the outside of a text that influences a reader, such as reviews, author websites, interviews, and correspondence. The paratext includes both the peritext and epitext [Gross & Latham, 2017].) A third student, who had experience in computer science, helped classmates learn how to critically evaluate sources as they sought texts related to their selected domains of study. So students play active roles in designing our readers' workshop space, and even mini-lessons require their participatory efforts. We identify guest speakers in the community who might offer mini-lessons as well, and we specifically seek out opportunities to connect with members of the community to strengthen our collective goals for readers' workshop.

In the following vignette, Kelly Burns, a literacy curriculum facilitator, shares recommendations from her yearlong readers' workshop designed with intentional "learning laps" for students to deepen their reading. Her lap-based secondary readers' workshop is part of her spiral approach to learning that centers students. Kelly's approach to readers' workshop differs from how I structure my own readers' workshop; it's reader-focused rather than domain-focused, offering another approach you might adapt to your own context and purposes. Both approaches, although they differ substantially, start with the students.

Co-Constructing the Path to Critical Literacy in a Secondary Readers' Workshop

Kelly Burns
Secondary Literacy Curriculum Facilitator, Poudre School District, CO
Email: kburns@psdschools.org

We as teachers must pivot in our teaching practice to be more intentional and active critical literacy educators. The change must first take place in our own imagination of what literature is—and what it is not—and then in our canonical choices, our classroom libraries, our literacy instruction, our relationships, our ability to actively listen, our willingness to let some things die and rise from their ashes, and the active choice to reexamine how the structures of inequity in our pedagogy may be operating to maintain injustices or suppress liberated thinking and learning with our students. Our pivot is a reckoning, a truth-telling that can be articulated only after taking a long look at the small moments and big moves in our work with readers and writers.

Student agency and student ownership are two of the most important touchstones in a learning environment built on the foundation of critical literacy. We also know that to help our secondary students fall back in love with reading, or maybe fall in love with reading for the first time, we must creatively structure inclusive, accessible, and engaging reading experiences for them (Ehrenworth, 2020). We've known for some time, as noted by Allington (2002), that readers need (1) protected time to read, (2) access to books they find fascinating, and (3) expert instruction to help them grow as interpretive readers. We also know that as critical literacy teachers, we must co-create reading experiences so that the expert instruction portion of this three-pronged approach is truly shared and constructed *with our students, rather than for them.*

The intentional shifts we make as critical literacy educators to move toward student agency and ownership can take *many* forms. We can switch the books we teach or "allow" students to read, if we can find the funding for new ones. We can update our strategies. We can examine our language and relationships. We can shift our instruction to be more formative and feedback-based. We can make reading and learning tools more student-centered and student-owned. In this section, I suggest one important aspect of instruction where we can pivot, and that is taking an updated structural approach to readers' workshop in order to grow our readers into a more liberated and self-directed learning stance.

The following living and burning questions are lighting my way, giving me courage, and in general, what I've been thinking about lately and as a growing practitioner of critical literacy, is the philosophical foundation of the structural shift in readers' workshop into more intentional learning:

1. How can I work with students to examine what already exists in their imagination and experience, and use that to call them forth into growing our literacy learning in community?
2. How can I make pedagogical choices in structure, instruction, and speech that invite us to lean in together so that we might reshape what literature needs to be for us in order to grow?
3. How can I position students as the "great deciders" of whether a text qualifies as literature that is worth studying?
4. Chris Emdin (2019) empowers my students and me by insisting that "before we do the research, we must do the 'mesearch'." How might I teach this to my students as a constant literacy strategy so that it becomes second nature?

One powerful approach to working toward liberation and social change that honors true critical literacy instruction and that has life-giving growth for readers and a collective payoff for classroom communities is to run the lap-based secondary readers' workshop with student-based reading strategies and student-created reading tools for setting their own reading goals. This approach involves liberating the traditional structure of a workshop, liberating the strategies we use in the workshop, liberating the tools we ask students to use or create, liberating our teaching choices, and, finally, liberating ourselves from outdated assessment that assumes the onus to design instruction is on the teacher rather than the student. In this vignette, I focus solely on one shift, the lap-based readers' workshop, because it's the foundation for many of the other possible shifts educators might make.

(Re)designing a readers' workshop model into critical literacy learning laps asks the educator to create intentional and cyclical workshop structures that encourage reader agency rather than compliance. These cyclical structures emphasize scaffolded growth, from the reader's awareness of their current reading skills, into greater skill at interpreting texts, into deep knowledge of how to read texts and the ability to transfer that knowledge, which occurs when the reader can synthesize their mesearch, or life content and knowledge, with what they are reading. Quick pacing of lessons matters in this approach because we are *lapping*—a paradigm shift away from linear teaching sequences into a *spiral*. If students don't grasp the deep or transfer knowledge in their first lap of learning, that's perfectly acceptable. They will go around, again and again, with their *own* goals so that they can differentiate for themselves, being in what Eduardo Briceño calls "the learning zone" (2016). Planning learning laps requires critical literacy educators to plan in chunked units, which means four to five weeks of reading instruction (for yearlong, 180-day courses) in a deep dive, and then popping into four to five weeks of writing instruction in a deep dive. In every four- to five-week lap of reading and writing instruction, we hold ten- to twelve-minute mini-lessons, with the bulk of time devoted to reading and workshopping (e.g., partnering, building reading volume, collaborating, generous listening, filling our gaps with relearning, small groups, book clubs, partnerships), a time when we synthesize our thinking and self-monitor, and a time when we share and move forward. Of course, students will read and write in each unit, and read like writers and write like readers.

Lapping in Readers' Workshops

Readers' Workshops in Lap One: Building Volume and Stamina

In lap one of any reading unit, and especially at the beginning of any school year or course, we offer, encourage, and push independent reading with any choice books our students want and that are related to topics they are interested in learning more about. The goal of this structural lap in growing the deep reader toward liberation is to *build their volume and stamina while learning about their reading lives*. Volume and stamina mean pages, pages, and pages of reading. Jeff Wilhelm (2015) encourages us in this lap to "Let Them Read Trash." Why? He asserts that growing the pleasures of reading will pay off in an independent reading life for our students—they must learn to love their reading through any of the doorways of their choosing, and it isn't our right or responsibility to choose the door they walk through. When our readers build volume and stamina with books they love, they build confidence, and some of them acquire for the first time an identity as a reader. Again and again we discover that some of our students "fake read" (pretend to read challenging texts) when forced into a classroom novel. According to Mary Ehrenworth (2020), this first lap is a very short unit—about two to three weeks—so that we can learn, as we confer with our readers and watch their reading lives unfold, who they are in their own reading worlds. This approach is student-choice based, but we are gathering information in a formative instruction cycle of planning.

The mini-lessons for readers' workshops in this portion of the lap cycles all focus on students learning about their own reading lives and how those might connect to their lives as a whole and to their communities. It's exploratory, with excavation, exhumation, and excitement to motivate and move students in their volume of pages read and stamina to build attention and focus. It's the reading equivalent of narrative writing. In this portion, we are, as critical literacy teachers, fulfilling Allington's (2002) suggestions by protecting as much time as is humanly possible for students to read and helping them develop access and agency with books that excite them—all the while, learning about how we can adjust our teaching to student needs for the remainder of the learning process.

Readers' Workshops in Lap Two: Building Interpretive Reading Skills with Intention and Clarity

The second lap in this liberatory structure of reading units will fulfill Allington's third call to grow the reader, and that is to build their interpretive reading skills with intention and clarity. According to Kate Roberts (2018) in *A Novel Approach*, this lap consists of whole-class novel instruction that focuses on interpretive reading skills, instruction built into the daily readers' workshop. But this is also time to teach and learn together, through small groups and conferring, the skills that our readers showed us they need in lap one. We do both whole-class interpretive reading instruction here and partnered and small-group learning to dial-in on the skills readers need in order to move from surface to deep knowledge.

Students need to guide more of this learning lap than they did during the first lap.

Readers' Workshops in Lap Three: Book Clubs, Collaboration, Assessment

In this lap, we can hold book clubs, we can create products through projects, we can collaborate with the community. This is the true assessment lap. We ask ourselves, "Can a student move their own mesearch, combined with what we have learned in a whole-group context and in smaller groups or partnerships, out into the world?" This is the transfer portion of learning, and it is almost entirely student-centered and collectively created. Books clubs are the most manageable way to move into this portion of a liberated teaching structure, but project-based learning teachers may know this as "pushing into exhibition." The growth we helped students set goals toward should be evident here through what Guskey (2018) mandates as product, process, and progress.

Conclusion (for Now)

Who are we centering in our structural choices? Who might benefit from the linear sequence of our unit plans versus moving into a spiral of learning that is built on reciprocity, feedback, and recursive processes? How do we grow our readers into agency and action and ownership through a structure that asks them to be compliant? However you decide to make your small move forward in your teaching practice, you are indeed moving. There is no stasis in this work of teaching literacy. We are either slowly retreating from the needs of our students, our communities, and our profession or we are responding with actionable and intentional courage. Let's be on the side of courage so that we can model a progressive journey alongside our learners and honor the process as much as the product and progress we co-construct.

Whatever your model or approach to readers' workshop, the vast majority of time should be spent in activities such as independent reading, working in book groups, or working with peer groups on a shared domain to study. During this time, you might conference with students to identify their needs and interests. The readers' workshop process trusts in young people to take charge of their own learning. There is minimal teacher-directed time, and even when you or a student is the instructor of a mini-lesson, you don't take more than twelve minutes to do so. Sharing is a part of the collaborative process, so sharing some level of student progress in knowledge, goals, book recommendations, learnings and understandings, etc. adds to the classroom community and collaborative experience. There are no strict rules for how workshop time is structured; it often varies from class to class with the same teacher. Students might, for instance, instruct their mini-lessons from the board or in a circle of peers, to the entire class or in small groups. Guest speakers might vary throughout the day, and participation with the community might differ. The aim of this model is to foster independent and collaborative growth and to trust in our readers to co-generate a process that supports them.

Balancing Texts and Connecting with Students' Lives and Community

When considering all of these approaches for integrating texts into our communities of practice, we must also examine how our classroom community is balancing texts. Overall, a literary diet should demonstrate a range of intercultural and intracultural representation. When generating (and, one hopes, co-generating with students) a balanced curriculum, it is important to look at the entire semester or year and ask ourselves whose voices are and are not centered in the classroom. Including a token text that features a character from a minoritized population within a white, Eurocentric curriculum doesn't make our classroom's curriculum culturally affirming or engaged with community. Relegating texts to designated history or heritage months offers students a supplemental rather than a rich cultural experience. Curricula and classroom libraries should be expansive with different philosophies, ideas, and experiences (Oswald & Smolen, 2010). Students should be invited to think critically about the texts in their classrooms. As Rosenblatt (1938/1995) writes, "[I]n a democracy, the more varied the literary fare provided for students, the greater is its potential as an educationally liberating force" (p. 204). Tatum (2009) recommends building textual lineages—carefully chosen texts with significance for each student.

You might also examine overall text selection relative to the assumptions or beliefs it might reinforce. For instance, as Thein and Kedley (2015) explain, if a teacher uses only LGBTQ+ texts that conflate the coming-of-age trope with the coming out trope, students might assume that LGBTQ+ youth will be underdeveloped until they come out. Scholars offer instructional alternatives and approaches that have great potential in the classroom to actively work against stereotypes, deficit-oriented beliefs, and assumptions. For instance, Torres (2019) suggests using superhero texts like *All-New, All-Different Avengers Vol. 1* (Waid et al. 2016) to decenter the white superhero and allow all youth to position themselves as heroes who can make powerful changes in the world. In the following vignette, Morgan Jackson reflects on text selection and the impact of the stories we choose to share. Overall, a community of practice should evaluate whether the texts they are centering are reinforcing trauma narratives and consider how they can offer a more balanced selection of titles.

Diversity: More Than Just Black Characters

Morgan Jackson
Bishop Gorman High School, Las Vegas, NV
Twitter: @MorganJaxon702

YA literature is an opportunity for us to move beyond tokenism with texts while also broadening the lens through which we as teachers, educators, and librarians discuss college readiness and rigor. It's not enough to include books with Black characters. We must investigate what those characters are doing—or equally important, not doing. In looking at canonical literature, we can see that many of the Black characters are flat, static characters whose existence functions as a plot device to show growth or development in the main white character(s). Tom Robinson dies in *To Kill a Mockingbird* so that Scout can understand the horrors of racism. Although it's heralded as a great novel for discussing race, consider what it really shows about race. Tom isn't depicted as a fully realized human being. The community of the novel doesn't need his death to be made aware of its glaringly obvious racism, but Tom's fate is determined by the author as a way to progress Scout's development. His body is a commodity used to teach a young, white, teenage girl about race. Similarly, conversations about Huck Finn often center on Huck and how Jim impacts him or how Huck's time with Jim has changed Huck. Rarely does anyone ask how Jim is impacted by this time or his relationship with Huck. Again, the focus is on how a young, white character has grown or developed through their interaction with a Black character.

Each of us has the ability to determine what we expose our students to in the literature we make available and study. Even in the most scripted classrooms, we can offer in-class libraries, book talks about texts we've read, or other opportunities for students to encounter texts with characters that include the variety of lived experiences of people in our real world. Those of us who select our own curriculum don't have to give up a rigorous reading list to create a diverse one.

Rigor as an educational idea says we challenge our students and push them to challenge themselves. In a lot of ways, modern YA literature provides students with the same opportunities as canonical texts. Shakespeare, Chaucer, *Beowulf* all appear on numerous high school reading lists because of what many see as a chance for students to engage with complex texts and language. For example, debates rage about Shakespeare's use of poetry and prose to reflect on the status of the speaker. But books like Elizabeth Acevedo's (2018) *The Poet X* and L. L. McKinney's Nightmare-Verse trilogy *A Blade So Black* (2018), *A Dream So Dark* (2019), and *A Crown So Cursed* (anticipated 2023) provide the same opportunities that a Shakespearean play does for students to discuss dialect and word usage and to analyze an author's thought process in determining how characters speak in specific situations, formats, and places. *Beowulf* is rife with symbolism and invites a conversation about Christ imagery. Just as Kwame Mbalia's (2019) *Tristan Strong Punches a Hole in the Sky* is full of allusions to African lore and symbolism that can be analyzed and discussed. Chaucer is heavy on characterization and provokes discussion about how the characters' descriptions in the General Prologue and their individual tales reflect on the traveler. In a similar vein, Tomi Adeyemi's Legacy of Orisha series, *Children of Blood and Bone* (2018) and *Children of Virtue and Vengeance* (2019), follows travelers on a pilgrimage to a holy land, providing plenty to analyze in terms of who the characters are, what is expected of them, and what they do and learn on their journey. Everything we do with canonical texts can also be done with modern YA (or middle grade) texts, and with novels featuring a Black main character who isn't experiencing violence.

It's also important to move beyond carnage and dependence on Black trauma to tell a story. In recent years, Nic Stone's (2017) *Dear Martin*, Jason Reynolds and Brendan Kiely's (2015) *All American Boys*, Reynolds's (2017) *Long Way Down*, and Angie Thomas's (2017) *The Hate U Give* have made it into classrooms and onto reading lists across the country. While this is an improvement in the all-too-white literary curriculum, there is still an undue focus on the victimization of Black bodies, Black men specifically. The Blackness of the character is often necessary to the plot of the story, and when that happens, the character ceases to exist as representative of the world outside of the novel and instead exists solely as a catalyst to drive the novel. While such stories are necessary and beneficial, especially when written by Black authors telling their authentic truths, it's still imperative to be aware of the ways in which we present groups who are already marginalized in society.

Representation matters. Schools treat the contributions of white people in literature as foundational, and students absorb that lesson. Text suggestions and exemplars are full of white kids who explore new worlds, go on adventures, solve mysteries, create their own businesses, fall in love, and come of age. So white kids grow up reading about people who look like them doing all of these things, thus learning they too can do all of those things. Through this exposure, we all grow to see white people as autonomous beings, in a variety of situations and circumstances, capable of doing anything, going anywhere, while Black people remain mere bodies that things, often violent, happen to. We learn to expect these things from literature and life, and our brains absorb these images as the norm.

The stories we share with our students will have an impact on how they view and interact with the world around them. Whether we know it or not, they internalize the messages they get from these stories. What plays out on the nightly news and in discussions on social media is a direct result of the severe inequity entrenched in our educational system and literature. YA literature is an opportunity to change what the next generation is hardwired to believe about themselves and each other. Although it's easy to focus solely on Black and white characters, these ideas should be applied to all populations. Lack of exposure creates ignorance, which often manifests as anger or fear. Providing books that reflect on all people's lived experiences will help to demystify the unknown and remove the label of "other." Anti-Muslim and anti-immigrant sentiments so apparent in contemporary culture can be reduced and eradicated in future generations if we expose our students to books with Muslim and immigrant characters

> who are living everyday experiences in which their religion or citizen status isn't the focal point of the book.
>
> There is power in the texts we expose our students to. Power to change the current reality of students who are marginalized by allowing them to see themselves in a story. Power to change the reality of students who have limited exposure to those who live or identify differently than they do. And the power to ensure that the kids in our sphere of influence grow to appreciate the similarities and differences of all people and acknowledge the humanity of everyone.

Examining and Selecting Texts

A lack of confidence and fears about controversy and censorship prevent teachers from varying their text selection (Nilsen et al., 2012; Bishop, 1992). If you experience this paralysis, know that you are not alone, and that there are strategies you can use with students to evaluate and make determinations about an author's authority and a text's authenticity.

Poor representation in books sends a message to children that they are not valued in society. In an effort to become critically conscious, publishers initially responded to calls for more diverse texts and characters with tokenism (e.g., changing a character's name from Mary to Maria or inserting a "minority" character in the place of a white character in an original version) (Smith et al., 2016). The texts that we feature in our classrooms should offer rich stories reflecting lived experiences and be culturally and linguistically conscious. There isn't a checklist for representation, but there are evaluation strategies and resources available that offer considerations for text selection. When thinking critically about the texts you could potentially use in your classroom, you might examine writing and illustrations for stereotypes and language, analyze dialogue and the message it might send to readers, consider whether cultural and social issues are portrayed accurately and realistically, evaluate whether the text offers frank but not simplistic portrayals of problems, and question how the characters are positioned within the texts (Landt, 2006). More holistically, it's important to consider the values a book transmits and the way a culture is represented as a whole (Harlin & Morgan, 2009). Tatum (2009) provides a rubric to assist educators with identifying texts. He critiques disabling texts, which reinforce negative stereotypes, and praises enabling texts, which promote action. Enabling texts liberate and empower young people—they don't stress a victim mentality, and they provide platforms for change. Students should be encouraged to interrogate injustice; they should be permitted to act on these feelings of negativity in order to work toward an equitable, just society (Oswald & Smolen, 2010). The inclusion of contemporary themes (or historical themes with contemporary application) offers opportunities for teachers and classrooms to act from a platform that challenges injustices and the status quo in transformative ways.

As I note many times in this book (particularly in Chapter 5), the best way to evaluate texts is to read, read, and read and to listen carefully to experts. Building your knowledge of the high-quality books available for adolescent readers can only make you a better teacher of reading. It allows you to better match books with kids. An immersion in multicultural literature builds personal, reflexive awareness and allows you to become a more informed educator (Gay, 2000). Teachers who read widely are more likely to engage in rich literary conversations and to contextualize multicultural literature for their students. Reading and exposure to different perspectives and quality literature allows both adult and adolescent readers to become more aware of recurring themes that will help them select new texts (Bishop, 1992). This is an iterative process that requires time, commitment, and persistence (Gay, 2000; Ward, 2010), and the process never ends. There is no expert in the field who understands all human experiences, and scholars of young adult literature and English education depend on one another collectively to share their knowledge. When you read, you and your students might ask questions such as:

- Whose story is this?
- Whose story is being silenced?
- Whose story is being heard?

These are questions we might write on our walls to remind us as we plan to listen to these voices and to interrogate who we are and are not hearing. If we allow ourselves to become paralyzed by text selection and sit in the comfort of a traditional classroom library, we are preventing our students from hearing the voices that have been and are currently being silenced. The classroom then remains a teacher-directed room with four impermeable walls and titanium bars, and students are not encouraged to act in empowered ways to knock on hegemony's (big, heavy) door or test the strength of the bars.

As you evaluate texts with these strategies in mind, I encourage you to seek other supportive resources. Community members, scholarship, award recipients, and cultural insiders can all help with evaluating texts, because "good liberal intentions are not enough" (Delpit, 2006, p. 45). In Chapter 5, I share award lists, booklists, and review blogs that offer myriad book suggestions and recommendations for teachers and students. These lists provide a place to continue our learning as we listen to others who are committed to this work.

Censorship and "Controversial" Topics

A primary benefit of a community of practice is that the students are driving the instruction. Regardless of how we position ourselves as stewards, we are accountable when controversy arises. There is likely a topic that makes your stomach churn when you consider the pushback you might receive from your department, administration, or parents/caregivers, and this topic seems to vary by community context. I will stand up *every time* for what my community of practice has co-determined to be best for their learning. Although students should be allowed to speak up for what is right too, I never place them in a vulnerable position. So if there are any consequences to them for speaking out, I stand up, and I speak loudly for their rights and intellectual freedom.

I intentionally tackle the issue head-on, and I am fearless. This stems from my commitment to disrupting texts in the classroom, but it also stems from personal experience. When I was in tenth grade, my English teacher began a class period mid-semester by asking us to return the book we were reading. We were halfway through the book. In a state of confusion, we passed back the books and signed off their return on book cards. We later learned from an op-ed in our local newspaper that the parent of a student in a different section of the course had called the principal to object to the text, and the principal had elected to stop instruction of the text (mid-book!) for all students in the tenth grade. I remember feeling gutted and that my rights as a student to read a text had been stripped by this parent. One parent's outspokenness censored the book for the entire school, and this parent went on to censor other books in the school in subsequent years. Caregivers can decide that a book may not be appropriate for their specific child, but there is no reason one parent should control a school district. Censorship negates professional trust in teachers, and it negates trust in students to put down texts they don't feel ready to read.

Teachers regularly demonstrate how they address censorship directly and explicitly. Some teachers have collaborated with students on units during Banned Books Week (bannedbooksweek.org) to explicitly and loudly address censorship with students, teachers, and the community. In the following vignette, Brooke Bianchi-Pennington shares a co-generated assignment sheet for a censorship podcast, which allowed her students to engage with others in their community to think deeply about and talk back to censorship in bold ways.

Censorship Podcast Assignment

Brooke Bianchi-Pennington
Hardin Valley Academy, Knoxville, TN
Twitter: @HVABBP

In passionate discussions about censoring materials for children and young adults, we often hear from parents, teachers, librarians, authors, and school board members—but not the actual people whose reading practices are being censored. This assignment speaks to that divide and invites students to create a podcast on the topic of censorship.

The Assignment

Students decide what is important to talk about in groups of three to four. They begin by creating a list of questions or topics their specific group is interested in. Some ideas they might want to think about include:

- Specific banned books that they have read and enjoyed
- What kinds of books get banned and why that is unfair
- What teens experience in real life vs. what gets censored
- Equity, diversity, and inclusivity as it connects to censorship
- How they think choices should be made about what gets put in a school library or on school/classroom reading lists
- Anything interesting they learned in class discussions about censorship
- Relevant research about censorship
- Censorship of the books they have read in their classes

As a class, we look at the NPR Podcast Challenge, to which they submit their completed assignments. This website offers tips, strategies, instructions, and other helpful resources for students to learn about the medium and prepare their projects: www.npr.org/2018/11/15/650500116/npr-student-podcast-challenge-home. Below is a sample rubric that students and I have developed for this assignment:

Element	Description	Points	Notes
Content	The student takes part in each conversation on the podcast with thoughtful responses.	/30	
Outside Resources	The student uses outside resources/research in discussion.	/30	
Organization	The podcast has clear segments that are introduced with smooth transitions. This includes appropriate introductions and conclusions.	/15	
Attention to Audience	While the tone of the podcast may be informal if the group chooses, there is still a sense of respect for the audience, with minimal cross-talk, clear voices, and no inappropriate laughter.	/15	
Audio Quality	It is obvious that editing has been done to eliminate silences or blips and unnecessary background noise. Effects or music has been edited in where appropriate with proper licensing.	/10	

The results of this project vary from year to year based on the emphasis placed on different aspects. For instance, the first year we took time to delve into podcasts as a medium, and students listened to different podcasts as exemplars. The podcasts that year had a more polished and structured feel and followed elements the students identified in the exemplars. The second year we spent more time talking about actual censorship because our state legislature was about to vote on a bill to form parental advisory boards to oversee library collections. This year we brought in a local librarian to talk about the issue, as well as took time to write our legislators. This crop of podcasts was less polished but more passionate as students saw an urgency in the discussion. In all years, the issue is one that gets students talking, specifically when they see which books have been challenged. Often the most fruitful part of the conversation in these projects centers on specific books that students are defending. The nature of the podcast allows this discussion to be both personal and also geared to an audience. It allows for a good balance between a normal discussion and a presentation. In a formal presentation, students tend to be more robotic; in an informal discussion, they are less deliberate. A podcast allows for a mix of planning and improvisation that is useful and feels more authentic.

Every classroom is political, whether or not we want to admit it. A classroom that focuses on white authors sends a political statement. An education that never features a character who identifies as LGBTQ+ sends a political (and personal) statement about what we value. Centering (and silencing—unintentionally or not) certain voices demonstrates what we value. Garcia and Dutro (2018) state, "We need to locate the political in our work, and locate ourselves within it. We need to find places to highlight how classrooms are spaces of inclusion and oppression, are spaces that value and actively resist diverse identities, histories, and knowledges" (p. 382). I urge my teacher candidates to work in school systems that will support them in their pedagogical approaches, and if this isn't possible, I encourage them to be the change they wish to see in the school (and the world). This means having honest dialogue with colleagues, department chairs, and administration about honoring the children in the classroom, community, and world. It might mean adjusting book policies. It might be co-envisioning civic possibilities or how youth can become involved in politics (Mirra & Garcia, 2017). If we are unsure how to take risks, we should find partners—in person or virtually (see Chapter 5)—who *are* sure, and lead classrooms with confidence and with these partners by our side as a collective force.

Sometimes minor and intentional shifts in school or department written policies beget confidence. I taught in a high school that had a book policy stating that any newly introduced whole-class text required a parent or caregiver letter home. If no parent or caregiver contested the new book for three years, no letter was needed in subsequent years. Parents and caregivers were permitted to opt out of any book for an alternative, but they had to write a summary justifying their reasoning for opting their child out of instruction, and we encouraged parents and caregivers to read the books and share their reasoning. Schools are democratic places and spaces for learning, and reading outside of a white, heteronormative, cisnormative, monolinguistic experience should not be controversial.

Parents and caregivers served as partners in my classroom, and I sent home a letter at the beginning of the school year to encourage them to reach out to me to discuss their child's education. This letter included a list of the titles and descriptions of whole-class and literature circle texts. It also included a description of my classroom library, which contained hundreds of books. In the letter, I explained that I trusted and encouraged students to choose texts based on their own level of readiness, and a parent or caregiver could be involved in this process if they felt it was necessary. If this policy didn't work for the parents or caregivers of my students, I enthusiastically invited them to come to my classroom to help select independent reading texts for the school year with their child. No one ever took me up on this offer, and I never did have a censorship issue regarding my classroom bookshelves. It was hard to argue with a bookshelf and a classroom experience when the students chose the books themselves and when I gave parents and caregivers the opportunity to peruse the bookshelves at any point in the year. Opting out of whole-class texts required caregivers to discuss their concerns with me along with alternative text options for the child. I was willing to substitute the text and assignments with options that offered the same high level of thinking. I invited parents and caregivers to request copies of books to read in advance or alongside students, and I urged them to share their thoughts or concerns about the texts. At the bottom of the letter, I asked them to sign their agreement to allow students to read and listen to books or provide their own reading.

If you find yourself in a situation with a censorship issue, there are resources available to you. The NCTE Intellectual Freedom Center (https://ncte.org/resources/ncte-intellectual-freedom-center/) offers position statements, like the *Statement on Academic Freedom*, *Guidelines for Dealing with Censorship of Instructional Materials*, and other supportive materials to demonstrate professional justification for your case. They have also culled a list of supportive statements from authors and offer a way for teachers to report censorship incidents and seek support. The American Library Association offers other resources on intellectual freedom (www.ala.org/advocacy/intfreedom), including a Library Bill of Rights, a peer-reviewed journal, and statements connecting the First Amendment and censorship.

Conclusion

As evidenced by the multiple instructional options described in this chapter, communities of practice can be implemented in existing courses and curricula in a multitude of ways both large and small. Whatever combination of approaches you employ, students benefit from your willingness to take a step back to allow their interests, or domains, to take center stage in the design process—a process developed with the students. The process should be collaborative and trust in students to make decisions that impact their reading lives. Course (re)design should be managed either as a whole class with a shared domain or with smaller groups within the class—building and sustaining readers and thinkers and situating instruction in authentic ways. The students can develop practices that are outward-facing and meaningful to their communities or for global audiences. All of the approaches to course design described here can be implemented in ways that rattle the cage—

either by slipping practices through the bars as a first step or by breaking down the bars entirely in revolutionary ways. You know your context, community, and students. I challenge you (and hope you will, in return, challenge me) to rattle the cage even harder tomorrow.

Chapter Four

More Hands in Stand-Alone YA Literature Courses

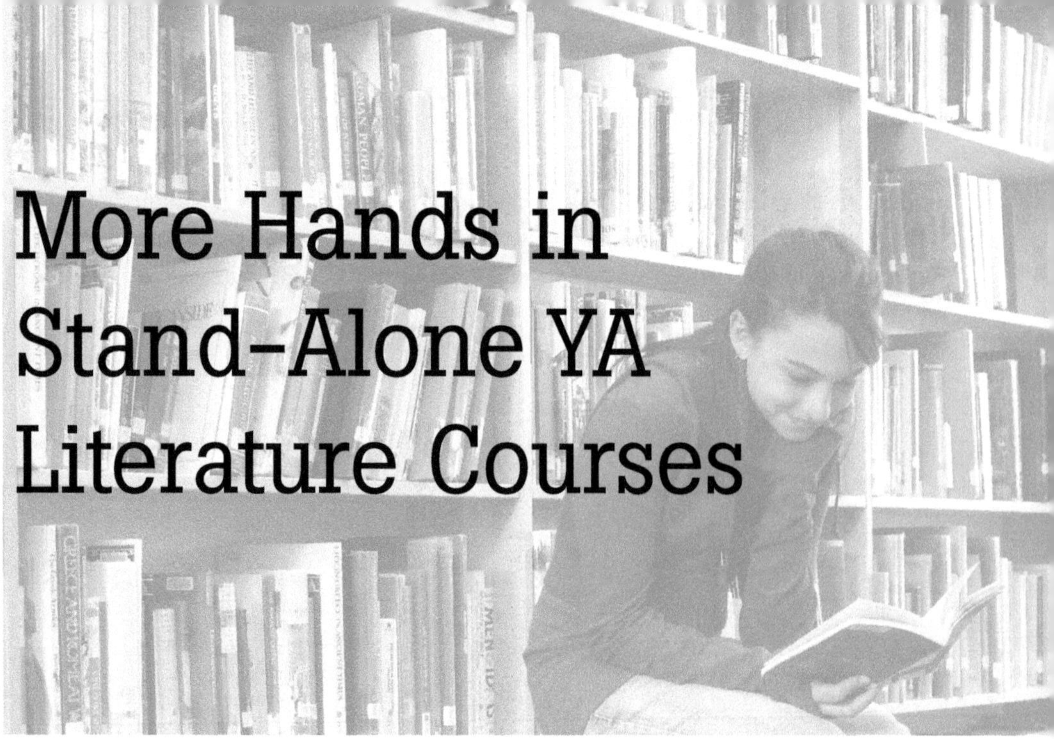

We walked into the bookstore and their eyes glistened. The book fair they'd hosted collaboratively had raised money to purchase "fresh" bean bags, a comfy reclining chair, dozens of sets of books, and hundreds of bookmarks and swag for our classroom. But this field trip was what they were most excited about—permission to walk into the bookstore as a united front to ask the questions they most wondered about. I stood back and watched them in action.

One group stood in front of the store manager of the young adult section. They had notebooks in hand to conduct more research on their inquiry-based project and were prepared to share their findings with their peers the following week.

> *"How do you decide which books to put on the shelves?"*
>
> *"Do starred reviews and book awards play a big role in which books you order?"*
>
> *"Do you consider representation and inclusivity when you order books?"*
>
> *"Who decides which books face forward on the shelves?"*
>
> *"Does your store respond to trends in the news and market?"*

Another group of students took notes as they examined the shelves of young adult literature and peered closely at the covers and critically analyzed the displays. They were curious about what was (and wasn't) offered in the section. A third group was doing a quantitative study—cataloging book covers with the Youth Lens (Petrone et al., 2015) as a theoretical framing for their work.

Each small group was prepared and focused. Following our class discussions of trends and starred reviews, students had workshopped inquiry-based research studies based on the questions they had wondered. They asked questions that were difficult to answer within the walls of our classroom. Their hard work in the student-run book fair funded and supported the trip to seek answers to their questions. When we returned to class, they would gather their findings and formulate public-facing products to share with peers in the class and community. These included Tumblr pages, signs across town, bookmarks they placed inside the covers of texts at the bookstore, and letters to and communication with local bookstores. The trip to the bookstore was one piece of their research.

I start this chapter with a vignette from one iteration of my young adult literature elective because for me, the freedom within this course's design is the ultimate way to put students' domains, or interests, first. The students asked for a class that allowed them to read more—and thus, learn more. Before I delve into my conception and the realization of the stand-alone YA literature course—a secondary school course devoted solely to the study of young adult literature, the domain defined by my students whom I'd had in previous courses—I share the words of the students who ultimately enrolled in the course. Their suggestions drove me to create this course, and without their ideas and collaboration, the course (and this book) would not exist. They helped me consider whether the course should count as a requirement or an elective and which components were important, structurally, for the curriculum. Without their input and help, the course would not have succeeded. A university researcher, a teacher from another school, and I conducted a study of the course (Glenn et al., 2018; Glenn & Ginsberg, 2016), so I'm able to offer a window into students' thoughts through direct quotes from their interview responses. In the interviews, they were asked how the YA literature course benefited them, and they shared the following ways in which the stand-alone YA course:

- *Offered them time and space to read.* Dylan (all names are pseudonyms identified for the study) shared, "Usually [my English teacher] gives us maybe ten to fifteen minutes, and I just feel like it's not worth it, so, I mean, unless I have a good thirty plus minutes, um, I don't usually like to read." Kyra revealed, "In my YAL class, we have silent sustained reading [SSR], and that's the time I normally read because, when I get home, I do homework, I go to work, go home and do [more] homework, and then I really don't have time to read because I'm so tired."
- *Helped them find books.* Devontay shared how his reading habits benefited from the way the class was organized freely: "After I read a book [that I like], I look for the next closest book to that same exact plot and theme. . . . I think

[the elective is] more beneficial because, when you're in there, you're getting recommended books, and you're getting offered books that are actually interesting and actually want to make you read, like, they're catching interest, they look good, they look . . . interesting."

- *Taught some of them to become independent readers for the first time.* Aaron, who was also a student in my traditional English course, was lured by the classroom library. He admitted, "I was sitting right next to the bookcase, so I would always pick up a random book. [. . .] Then I started reading on my own, like, last year. Eleventh grade."
- *(Re)ignited their love of reading.* Jordyn shared, "I've always kind of wanted to read, but I never thought I had the chance to read. [The YA Lit] class is really fun because we have silent sustained reading where we can just sit and read. I just want to get back into reading books, and that class has really helped, I think." Neil, who was a student in a different, traditional English class with me, said, "Yeah, Mrs. Ginsberg read. She had a huge library in the back, and that is why I started getting back into it."
- *Was responsive to their reading needs.* Nia, a student the school labeled as struggling and at risk of dropping out, shared, "You get to pick whatever book you are interested in, and you get to read it at your own pace. So it's not like, 'Oh, you have to read Chapter 7 by tomorrow.' I'm a really slow reader, and I have a lot of issues with reading, so when I have a specific time, it puts more pressure on me and makes it a lot more difficult for me to read. . . . But when there's no specific time, I tend to read better and faster and more efficiently."
- *Was a course they looked forward to.* Nia shared, "Another thing I like about that class is the projects. Instead of them being, like, 'Oh, you have to write an essay on this book,' they're more like fun projects, projects that kids would want to do. Like book covers. We just finished doing the book covers, and that was, that was fun. And then we had, like, mini-book projects that we did. Just all of this stuff is really fun about that class. It's not one of those classes where it's like, when English class comes, you're dreading it, like, 'Aww, I have to sit in this class for eighty-four minutes, and it's just gonna be terrible.' When you go to Young Adult Lit, it's like 'Yes.' It's like, 'Finally, this class is here. I get to read.'"
- *Connected them to other readers.* Julia, said, "I just didn't know that that many people liked to read books too, and, like, wanted to learn about books."

Conception of This Course: Responding to a Need

After integrating several of the strategies described in Chapter 3 into my existing sophomore courses, I was pleased with students' increased commitment to reading and discussing literature. I wanted to build on this success, particularly given that too many students who advanced to the eleventh-grade American Literature and twelfth-grade British Literature courses in my school reported that they no longer had enough time to read on their own and maintain their independent reading habits. I'd seen the integration of YA literature work really well with students as sophomores, but when I chatted with the same students the following year in the hallways and after school in my classroom, they repeatedly bowed their heads and admitted, "I just don't have the time to read anymore." These were the same students who had read forty to fifty YA novels during their sophomore year, but now they seemed trapped by the required readings in their American Literature course. Most disturbing, they admitted that they weren't even reading those required texts. After working hard to develop and foster a love of reading and a steady exposure to recent YA literature with my sophomores, I felt like I'd been gut punched. Most of all, I was saddened because I knew that reading the young adult texts allowed them to engage in rich, relevant discussions about contemporary topics.

The curricula in our junior and senior English courses contained so much material and required reading that some colleagues admitted they were pressed to cover the mandatory material and thus were unable to incorporate YA literature at all. Although they valued the use of young adult texts at upper grade levels, they felt that it just didn't fit into the existing curricula. I offer no judgment about this because I had worked with the same rigid curricula and knew the limitations. Instead, this pushed me to think about some of the approaches I describe in the previous chapter. My colleagues and I talked about ways we could all make YA literature fit, but a brief integration of contemporary YA titles into existing courses didn't feel like enough for us. It still felt as though the mandatory materials were being privileged in ways that didn't break the hegemonic status quo of centering canonical texts. Given the school-level constraints and drawing on a suggestion from students, I began to explore the possibility of creating a stand-alone course dedicated to the reading and study of big questions (domains) that could be connected with YA literature and grounded in a commitment to student choice, autonomy, and community. This new course would be committed to critically exploring the world through inquiry related to student domains. We would interrogate our conceptions of ourselves as readers, read and critique YA texts, analyze constructions of reading in schools and the field of YA literature itself, explore contemporary topics of interest, foster (or introduce) a love of reading, and build/increase reader stamina. I should be clear that while I was excited about creating a stand-alone course that responded to student-expressed needs, I remained equally committed to tackling concerns about the privileging of canonical texts in other, existing courses, and my colleagues shared this same commitment.

The stand-alone course didn't focus on integrating YA literature alongside an existing curriculum. Instead, it was designed to allow students to define domains of study and to explore their interests through the reading of YA lit. Although young adult literature was central to much of what we did in this course, we were more focused on the time and space to explore ourselves as readers and thinkers and consumers of the literature and the world. It was grounded in my philosophy that learning and reading are at their best when we are given freedom, when our needs are met in responsive ways, and when we are courageously critical of the world around us. For some students, the stand-alone course simply gave them permission and space to research their passions and read voraciously. For others, the course gave them the connection they needed with peers to strengthen their readerly worlds. And for yet others, the space offered no judgment and allowed them to enjoy an exploration of domains and reading in ways they didn't associate with traditional structures of English courses. For all, the course allowed them time and space to delve deeply into domains, or contemporary topics they wanted to explore through literature. The course encouraged students to be critical of structures, including educational structures; critical of the ways in which equity, diversity, and inclusion are taken up in texts and in the world; and critical of the ways in which they saw themselves and others in the literature they read (again, see the Youth Lens in Petrone et al., 2015).

Many of these students had been enrolled in my traditional grade-level required English course. We talked about domains of interest and read YA literature in those courses as well. Yet there was something different and magical about this course, which stood alone by offering a critical freedom for all of us to explore whatever domains we were interested in exploring, and with no boundaries or standardized expectations.

My concept of critical freedom is layered and connected to the ideas I've raised thus far in this book about communities of practice. Freedom was critical for the course's success, to allow it to be centered on student interests (domains) and free of demands like standardized assessments (but supportive of other kinds of assessment—that is, *practice*, in the parlance of communities of practice). I was fortunate that my school respected my knowledge and expertise as an educator to co-design the course with students in a way that the students and I thought would allow them to be most successful. Another layer to this critical freedom was my students' freedom to ask critical questions of the world and of the field to stretch their thinking and research beyond the classroom. Students freely and critically analyzed the books they were reading, their own reading habits and approaches, and the ways in which reading was taught in schools. They asked big questions that pushed outside of the traditional limits of the classroom. *My* freedom was critical for the students to have their own critical freedom to make the course a meaningful experience for them as readers and thinkers.

With extensive flexibility in a stand-alone course, we can focus intently on fostering a love of reading with appropriate pedagogy. As the NCTE position statement (2018) affirms, "Teaching children's and young adult literature is about more than getting students to fall in love with reading. Preservice teachers also need to learn appropriate and effective strategies for helping students find books that will engage them as readers and as participants in critical, significant conversations about their lives" (xvi). This chapter offers suggestions for building and increasing autonomy and responsiveness in stand-alone courses that focus exclusively on YA literature—and to do so in a way that ties into the notion of communities of practice. The stand-alone YA literature course brings an exciting level of freedom for students and for us as teachers. Students are granted the freedom to co-design the course to engage with the field and offer their own critical perspectives on literature and scholarship. Within the course design and instruction, students have many opportunities to use their voices and read loudly.

More Hands (a Metaphor)

In Chapter 3, I offered a metaphor to think about how we integrate young adult literature into schools. I invited you to rattle the cage—consider what practices are held within the hegemonic bars of the cage and how you might slide texts, methods, and practices through the bars as a way to rattle them until they fall down. In this chapter, I offer the metaphor of hands (see Figure 4.1). About ten years ago, when I was getting ready to propose my stand-alone YA lit course to the Board of Education, I was brainstorming with a friend about the potential freedom and openness of a co-constructed course design with students. My friend asked, "Are you worried it will get out of hand?" I smiled conspiratorially with her and said, "I'm hoping it *will* get out of hand!" This was a course that, if done right, would feel like organized chaos. Students would become part of a community of practice, choosing almost everything in the class from the course structure to the texts to the design, and they would primarily be reading texts in self-defined groups or on their own. Their groups and the experience would be completely dynamic in response to their needs as learners and their domains of interest. We would think about our community often and consistently analyze how to make it stronger. We wouldn't be satisfied with the assessments (the practice) at the beginning of the course. Instead, we would develop and refine the practices as we learned more about our domains and evolved as learners. The course would get out of (my) hand and into *their* hands. We would co-generate and develop the course almost in its entirety. As steward, I would develop plans that guided our development and thinking about how we would design the course together, but I would intentionally decenter myself as we worked together to meet their interests and needs.

For this course to "get out of hand" and into the students' hands, I needed the helping hands of others. My Board of Education had to listen to the students

Figure 4.1. More hands metaphor.

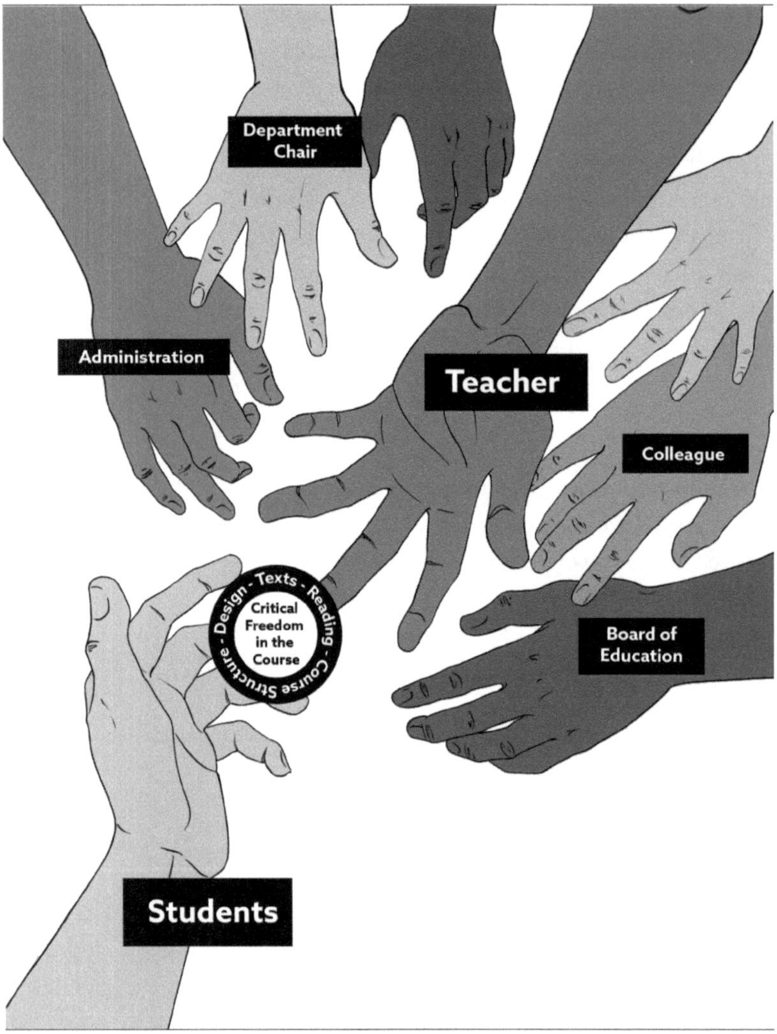

(who attended the meeting to advocate for the course) and to our hopes for the course. They did, and they offered funding. My administration had to trust me to co-generate its design with students. They did, and they expressed a willingness to stand by me if needed. My department chair had to be supportive of my vision. She actively encouraged it, and she even graciously managed to find me funding to purchase texts the students had identified as desirable. My students would have to trust me in this organized chaos and have to move away from a grades-based approach toward a learning-based approach. They did, and we co-designed the course you'll read about in this chapter. The course got out of (my) hand and into the hands of others.

Stand-Alone Courses as Requirements or Electives?

An important consideration in the development of a stand-alone course is how it will fit into course sequencing. You might choose to offer a course like this as fulfilling graduation requirements, primarily as an option for a mandatory, grade-level course, while others might offer the course as an elective. I have seen both options in action and while both offer strengths, I encourage you, if possible, to propose and defend the course as an elective, offered in addition to existing requirements. The elective format is often strapped to fewer curriculum-based school- and district-level requirements and thus allows you to more flexibly design course content and instruction to support individual student needs and interests. Additionally, as an elective the course isn't likely to be subject to standardized tests and other departmental and school requirements. (Even though decades of research repeatedly demonstrate that students whose reading habits are nourished will acquire and build on the skills often assessed on such tests [Cunningham & Stanovich, 1998; Fisher, 2009].) Often, classes organized in this way enroll students of varying ages and skill levels, allowing for a great diversity of readers and experiences, as well as rich classroom discussion.

The elective format does, however, have drawbacks. First, an elective YA literature course might be perceived by your school and students as less important, as merely supplemental to core curriculum and courses. This stance can be countered once YA literature is tightly interwoven into other courses and teachers, parents, and students begin to see its value (see Chapter 3). Second, an elective might also be the target of course cuts during budgetary reductions, especially if it's perceived as less important. Further, students are less likely to enroll in an elective course if it isn't required, and they may view the course as an additional English class that places unnecessary demands on them and their already busy schedules. And finally, given the wide array of students attracted to and enrolled in YA literature courses, you may feel pressure to lower the demands of the coursework to maintain interest in an elective. I argue that you can combat this pressure by designing an elective that is both substantive and appealing, one that celebrates students and their interests by differentiating and individualizing instruction. My course, for example, enrolled only twelve students during its first semester of implementation, but by the third year, I was teaching two full sections of the course (twenty-eight students in each section) and offering an advanced YA literature elective, which drew from multiple course sections and allowed for fascinating discussions because a new but overlapping community of practice had formed.

I found that, given their willingness to sign up for the course as an elective, the students passionately enjoyed reading or wanted to rediscover their love of reading. Working with young people who genuinely enjoyed reading or wished to become better at it afforded me opportunities for more creative instructional methods because student engagement was high. It's important to note that students who traditionally enrolled in my YA literature electives were not necessarily students also enrolled in honors courses. On the contrary, my students were enrolled in all levels of English courses. This affirms what we know to be true—that all students at all levels of instruction can love reading, despite the deficit labels and assumptions placed on them (Glenn et al., 2018). Students enrolled in my course reported that they decided to take the course because they enjoyed reading or wanted more time in school to engage in reading or discussing contemporary issues; however, more than half were doing poorly in their regular English courses because of their unwillingness to read the assigned texts (Glenn & Ginsberg, 2016). This illustrates the need for a course that creates a space and place to embrace a love of reading without assumptions and without a prewritten set of standards that limits your and your students' freedom.

Although the elective format may be preferable because it allows for this freedom, any stand-alone course (required or not) will benefit students. Schools range immensely in their requirements and rigidity, so a required course in some schools might allow for significant freedom and be the best approach for you. It's important to weigh carefully the needs of the school and the students when deciding whether the stand-alone course should be offered as a requirement or an elective.

Overarching Course Design Options

Because course design depends on the needs and contexts of specific students in specific schools, I include the voices (the hands!) of teacher visionaries in the field who are doing stellar work with their students in stand-alone courses that integrate young adult literature. This chapter offers many ideas that are flexible and adaptable to the needs of different schools and classrooms.

I begin with my own approach. Each semester I used the core principles discussed in this chapter to shift course design and instruction to respond to my students' needs and encouraged them to co-construct the course by developing domains of interests, focusing on the community, and engaging in practice that connected locally and globally.

From the first day, I told students that they would help me design the course, and we would adjust its structure together and throughout the semester. We would engage in work that responded to their interests and examined contemporary issues (domains) along with conceptions of readers and reading. The following sections offer a wide variety of ideas that can be included or adapted according to the purposes of the course and student interest. In my course, to simplify and de-emphasize grading, I engaged in a constant feedback loop with students individually and as an entire class. In one iteration of the course, for instance, the semester's grades were determined by four elements that the students and I co-generated together. Each element was weighted and evaluated holistically at 25 percent of their total grade earned. These elements varied semester by semester, but in general, the four components were:

1. Whole-class work and evidence of practice
2. Small-group projects of practice (marking period 1) and independent passion/inquiry projects of practice (marking period 2)

3. Independent reading mini-projects and reading portfolios
4. Community and virtual connections

When students began the course, they shared domains they were interested in exploring, such as immigration, and we all shared titles they might explore related to these domains. They then formed book groups based on their interest in the particular domains they had co-generated. Groups had critical freedom to develop their practice, to choose their texts, and to determine the number of pages they asked one another to read each night. If the group disliked the text, they were invited (and encouraged) to put it down and select another. I trusted in my students and treated them as responsible readers. I met with groups regularly to talk about their domains and texts and joined intentionally as an additional reader rather than as a teacher in power. By decentralizing my power in the group dynamic, students felt trusted to have conversations about their domains and the texts in ways they would if they were reading the texts outside of the school setting. Each group worked to define their roles within the community. They thought about the strengths they could bring to the community and the ways the community could support them as readers and thinkers.

For the second marking period, we shifted the 25 percent of their weighted grade from book groups to choice independent reading and passion projects. This allowed students to remain within a community of practice but to work on their own interests and to refer back to their groups when they sought support. Some students continued to read in groups and meet as book clubs. The other 75 percent of their grade was consistent across the two semesters: mini-projects, reading conferences, virtual and community connections (see descriptions of learning experiences in the following Gathering Regular Feedback section).

Brooke Bianchi-Pennington offers an example of an overarching structure for a stand-alone course that differs from mine yet still allowed students critical freedom. Brooke shares the syllabus for her course (see the following vignette), an elective that, like mine, enrolls students who are also taking traditional English courses of all levels. The students and Brooke structured the course to focus on five overarching topics in young adult literature: the history of YA literature, censorship in YA literature, trauma in YA literature, the Youth Lens (Petrone et al., 2015), and the future of YA literature. Students read independent texts, longer texts, excerpts from texts, and shorter texts. They also viewed YouTube videos connected to the field of YA literature. Assignments included those that relate to the topics discussed, a class blog (and blog committee), a podcast submitted to the NPR student podcast challenge, and a final portfolio presentation.

Example of Assignments within a Stand-Alone Course

Brooke Bianchi-Pennington
Hardin Valley Academy, Knoxville, TN
Twitter: @HVABBP

Silent Sustained Reading (SSR): Each day in class we will spend the first fifteen to twenty minutes reading young adult books. Students must choose a young adult text of their own to read during this time, not an assigned text. This will be to help expose students to as much young adult literature as possible. This chosen text will be used in class to compare to other YA texts as well as to complete the outside reading book review.

Discussion: To foster organic discussion while balancing the need for evaluation and participation, for each unit, students will be responsible for participating in discussions.

Podcast: Students will work in groups to produce a podcast discussion surrounding a topic of their choice in young adult literature. This podcast will be submitted to the NPR student podcast challenge. You can read more about this here: www.npr.org/2018/11/15/650500116/npr-student-podcast-challenge-home.

***HVA Reads* Blog:** Beyond daily assignments in class, the major writing and project assignments will center on maintaining a Hardin Valley Academy class blog, *HVA Reads*. Some of the blog assignments will be developed by the students in committee. Some of the major established assignments for the blog are listed on the pacing guide.

Final Exam: The final exam for this course will be a portfolio presentation of the work each student has contributed to the blog along with a reflection piece on the process.

The assignments Brooke co-generated with her students center their interests. They participate in independent reading of choice, engage in discussions related to their interests, create podcasts for a topic of their choosing, maintain a public class blog, and generate portfolio presentations of their work for their final exams.

A third option for a course design—which I use with my college-level young adult literature course but that can be used at the high school level as well—is working with students to build a list of major topics in the field. We look first at new releases and award-winning titles to identify trends in the field. We then build a shared list of topics (domains) they are interested in exploring more deeply, and then we look for titles that align with their interests. Of note, this is one instance when I contribute a bit more heavily to the community of practice. As I explain in the next chapter, I'm committed to leading a literate life, and I try to read more than a hundred young adult titles each year, so I have an understanding of trends in the field. That said, my students are active readers and some read more books than I do. I strongly encourage them to contribute to the reading list.

As an example, this year my students wanted to talk about graphic novels as literature and critical visual literacy. Three of the books that students read were suggested by students who had made recommendations to me in the first few weeks of the semester: *Laura Dean Keeps Breaking Up with Me* (2019) by Mariko Tamaki and Rosemary Valero-O'Connell, *When Stars Are Scattered* (2020) by Victoria Jamieson and Omar Mohamed, and *The Magic Fish* (2020) by Trung Le Nguyen. These three books generated great discussions about critical visual literacy and using graphic novels in the classroom. But even further, our discussions as a community evolved, and we talked about three other topics: intersectionality, imagining, and authority and authenticity as they relate to story. Although we began with a topic in mind and the students spent significant time discussing that topic, our conversations evolved as we talked across texts. For their practice, which was related to their interest in improving English language arts classrooms, the students built unit plans to be shared publicly for teaching each of these texts through a critical visual literacy lens.

Every week we explore a different topic of interest as an entire class. We identify between two and four texts related to the topic, and students select a text most interesting to them and connected with that topic. At the college level, I don't even assign the students to book groups. Instead, I allow them to freely select the text that is most interesting to them, and I understand that we may have uneven group numbers. At the high school level, I check group numbers before students begin reading to ensure that I have enough texts for readers and that there are at least two students reading the same text. If a group feels too large and unwieldy, we split it into smaller groups discussing the same text. Although we spend just a week discussing each topic at the college level, you could stretch reading and discussions at the high school level to three- to four-week units.

Topics vary each semester, but my college students and I have co-generated topics to explore together, such as class, (dis)ability and the body, family and friendship, gender, death and dying, mental health, nonfiction, nontraditional forms of YA literature, the politics of adolescence, refugees and immigrants, sexuality, and young adults in other times and places. The topics we generate overlap significantly, and one benefit of this format is our ability to discuss how the topics intersect (and also differ across texts). For instance, in the week that we focused discussions specifically on analyzing family and friendship, students one semester selected between the texts *The Astonishing Color of After* (2018) by Emily X. R. Pan, *If I Ever Get Out of Here* (2013) by Eric Gansworth, *Piecing Me Together* (2017) by Renée Watson, and *They Both Die at the End* (2017) by Adam Silvera. These same books could easily be included in other topic discussions of the semester such as class, death and dying, mental health, and sexuality, among others. The community of practice may focus one week, for instance, on discussions of queer literature and related scholarship, but queer literature is also included throughout the entire course. Or we might focus literary conversations during Native American Heritage month, but we don't relegate Native American literature to the month of November. It should be everywhere in the course.

Students read one book related to the selected topic for each week and also complete 3,000 pages of free choice reading across the entire semester. The course components are co-designed, but they often include elements such as class participation, an independent project, a free choice reading portfolio (described in detail later), the leading of a small-group discussion on a student-generated topic for the week, and engagement (practice) with the local or global community.

If you're considering a stand-alone course, you and your students might try one of these three course designs or intersect and adapt these options in ways that work best for your classroom and your students. Whatever structural design you and your students decide on, though, consider how to involve students in these decisions.

Gathering Regular Feedback

As much as possible, students should also be in control of course content. With a continual feedback loop, instruction can be personalized to student needs. We can ask students to share anonymously (virtually and/or on exit slips) what is working and what could be improved within the community of practice. Students have used this space to suggest some of the forms of practice they'd like to see in the class. For instance, when we examined the marketing and design of book covers, a student wrote on an exit slip that she wished there was a class assignment to redesign unsuccessful book covers, a request that we enthusiastically honored. The students then wrapped their redesigned book covers around the books, wrote a brief justification on a note card, and created a display in the school library. One student elected to redesign a whitewashed cover (a character of color was depicted as white) and wrote why this was important. We checked, and the week after we made the display, students not enrolled in the course had signed out several of the books. When students know that their feedback is valued and taken into consideration within the community of practice, they become more active, engaged thinkers and participants.

Learning Experiences: Readings, Course Assignments, and Projects

Three of my goals for a stand-alone young adult literature course are to allow students the freedom and confidence to co-design a course related to their interests, expose ourselves to dozens of interesting titles (with peer suggestions valued highly too!), and allow for ample time to access and peruse texts. If these goals align with your interests, you might set aside a portion of the class period every day for shared brainstorming as a community of practice to check on your community and design next steps. You might also set aside time during which students can share the books they are reading with one another. In my class, this sharing process is informal and not graded, as this removes unnecessary pressure and makes the experience more participatory and less accountability-focused for students. Sitting in a circle with the students, we give book talks on our favorite texts and share titles. Together we decide how many titles we will each try to recommend throughout the course, and typically, my students have set an informal goal of each sharing at least three titles per semester. Those who read at a slower pace give talks on former favorites. During this sharing time, we also watch video book trailers for upcoming releases to generate interest in the newest offerings.

Below, I detail potential course assignments that have been successful in stand-alone YA literature courses (mine and those of others). Each is adaptable and flexible to the needs and interests of your community of practice. The students and I discuss potential assignments and weigh their individual needs along with the needs of their community. I've divided the course assignments here into three sections—whole class, small group, and individual learning, but of course these overlap and intersect in real life: whole-class work, for example, allows for independent, individualized learning opportunities, and individual work can be shared and workshopped with the class. So while this division is superficial, it allows me to explain more fully the myriad opportunities available to a community of practice within the design of a stand-alone course. In general, the communities of practice that I've worked with have found it best to start the year with a whole-class experience with a text we chose together, and then to move to book group experiences and then to end with independent learning. However, we wove in and out of whole-class, group, and individual learning throughout the semester to give students time to think collectively and to explore their own interests and passions.

Whole-Class Learning Experiences

To begin to create a sense of community among enrolled students at the outset of the course and help them define collectively the unique elements of their domain and its connection to young adult literature, students typically select a whole-class YA text of interest. Drawing on a shared text creates a common experience among participants and fosters opportunities to engage in discussion that can reveal student strengths and areas of concern; honest communication about books also helps students begin to build trust in us as teachers and in one another. During these experiences, I'm able to work with students individually around these strengths and areas of concern (see the later section about conferencing). The book might be shared in a read-aloud format (described in detail in Chapter 3), or groups of students might teach different portions of the shared text to increase their sense of ownership over the book and the course.

When students are invited to pursue their interests and develop their own reading paths, a one-text model typically doesn't continue beyond the first unit. I advocate for a model in which the majority of class time involves student book groups, independent reading, and dialogue in the community of practice, yet I also recognize some benefits of a one-text model as a supplement to the course. My students and I have never used more than one shared student-selected text in my YA literature courses because I don't believe one-text models encourage independence and taking responsibility for reading choices. I've never started my YA literature elective knowing which whole-class book the students will read. (One exception: when I've taught this course at the college level, I've had to preselect the first text due to financial aid and scholarship issues.) Assessment and evaluation emerge from mini-projects related to the text and our discussions. If my school requires that I give a reading quiz—which I am loathe to do because it feels punitive and authoritarian to me—I ensure that the "quiz" is an authentic reading assessment that connects to students, community, and the real world. For example, after reading a section of Renée Watson's (2017) *Piecing Me Together*, students spent some time designing a mentorship program that would be helpful to them and wrote a brief reflection on how this program compared to the Women to Women program described in the text.

Mini-Projects

Throughout a semester, small projects connected with domains, or topics of interest, for a shared text emerge. Opportunities for mini-projects often arise as students begin to think like readers and ask questions related to author's craft. The community of practice works together to co-generate mini-projects at the start of the semester, and we adapt them as the semester moves forward and interests evolve. Although I consider myself to be an organized planner, I have learned to design plans that foster authentic conversations that check in with the community to consider how we might develop a responsive, student-centered community of practice. One semester, students expressed interest in thinking about the effectiveness of book endings and what the public expects in book endings. At the time, there were strong debates about the endings of several popular books. We decided to spend time researching literature about book endings and considering motivations for ending books in specific ways and how this impacts readers and communities of readers. Students then worked in their book groups to consider the ending of the text they had read together—one that they felt didn't respond to realities in society or in their community, specifically. Following this analysis, the students selected a new text and rewrote the ending, specifically focused on responding to global realities. They used the literature we had gathered about strong book endings to inform their writing and reflect on the process. They then invited a key stakeholder in their community so they could share the endings and discuss how they differed and why it mattered.

Another semester, when we checked in on our community of practice, students shared that they were experiencing difficulty expressing their thoughts about the books they were reviewing on Goodreads (www.goodreads.com), a social networking website that allows students to post book reviews publicly and discuss book-related topics online. As a mini-project, the students selected exemplary book reviews for texts they had read and enjoyed, and as a community of practice, we evaluated the aspects that made the reviews successful. We also examined how and why certain reviews seemed to reach more readers and how to grow our audience, if desired. Examining the book reviews specifically, students identified quality elements concerning author's craft, and for their mini-projects, they rewrote or revised three book reviews they had already written to make them stronger. They then printed these reviews and placed them with the books we were selling through our Scholastic book fair fundraiser.

Every class of students is different in their interests and needs. Sometimes their needs are more focused on reading and writing, as described in the previous two examples, and when this happens, I ask students to consider the wider community. I ask them to think about aspects such as audience and connections to community. We work together to connect their projects to authentic audiences outside of the classroom and to consider how their projects are situated within local and global concerns. In the first example, the students were dissatisfied with endings because they felt the endings too easily dismissed a large social concern. In the second example, students felt that the books they were reading could be used as tools of protest, and they were frustrated that they didn't feel their reviews were "good enough" or reaching audiences in the ways they desired.

The tools we discuss also connect with the standards required of courses, even elective courses. For teachers who are considering how the state standards apply to the work of a community of practice, I invite you to share the pertinent standards with your community of practice—your students. They have identified practice (mini-projects) related to their domains, and they can adapt these projects, if needed, to easily connect to reading, writing, and communication standards. If we teach from our hearts, we invite students to share their needs and interests to build our courses. This work almost always meets the standards, and if it doesn't, we can easily adapt or tweak our work to make sure it does.

Discussions and Presentations Exploring and Critiquing the Field

One major thrust of my course is driven by my belief that my community of practice can be (if they aren't already) contributors to the field of young adult literature. A significant portion of our class time is dedicated to exploring the field. We look at the history of the field as well as past and current trends by reading blogs and articles from major library magazines and publisher websites; we talk about how books earn starred reviews, and how this influences the market; we follow book awards, examine their criteria, and look at past winners; and we examine critiques of and within the field. And then we consider how we can *be a part of* the field. This might include writing for public audiences or working with community partners to look at the ways we, as a community of practice, can make a change.

Together, we also look at scholarship within the field of YA literature. As a *steward* in the community of practice, it is my job to bring in opportunities for exploring scholarship. As a *member* of the community of practice, it is also my job to avoid telling students how we will use that scholarship in our classroom. Often, my students elect to work with peers or in small groups to select a scholarly journal article of interest to share with and present to the rest of the class. This allows them to explore a topic they are curious about, engage with scholarship, and practice their presentation skills. Because the language in scholarly articles can be difficult, pairing and grouping students offers a supportive structure. I include this activity in the whole-class section because we have typically worked to collaboratively identify articles and topics that we are interested in learning about, and students choose to explore their topics of interest and share their learning with the whole class. The articles we use are from *The ALAN Review*, the scholarly journal dedicated to young adult literature. Archived articles (excluding the last three years) are available online for free (https://scholar.lib.vt.edu/ejournals/ALAN/), and I also provide recent copies of the journal for students to peruse.

In this activity, students have typically read and studied their choice article and synthesized their learning into a slide (or some other presentation format) to share with our community of practice. Together we determine what these presentations will look like, but students have usually added an interactive component to their presentation to increase peer engagement with the content. For instance, one group of students chose to read and share Spiering's (2017) "Reviewing to Exclude? Critical Discourse Analysis of YA LGBTQ Book Reviews for School Librarians."

Spiering analyzes the language of book reviews of LGBTQ young adult literature to explore how this language might influence school librarians' decisions to include the literature in their collections. The students began their presentation by asking classmates to read a short book review cited in the article. They asked their peers to consider how the language in this book review might impact their decision to purchase the text if they were a school librarian. The interactive component of this presentation allowed students to think critically about equity and access and prepared the presenters to share Spiering's argument that we must "challenge and disrupt assumptions about youth that are hidden in [the] language" of book reviews and consider how this language affects access to and information about YA literature (p. 52). Considering the *practice* element of a community of practice, this kind of exploration invites students to participate in their own scholarship or exploration of a research topic of interest and share their learning in public domains.

Small-Group Learning Experiences

My students most often prefer to work together in small groups based on a common topic and text of interest. To begin, they don't think about the practice they will develop, but instead focus on the domain of interest and potential, related texts. During every class period, they meet in their book groups to discuss what they read, ask questions for clarity, and anticipate what might come next. A literature circle model can encourage group discussion, particularly between readers with little experience with student-led, small-group discussion. After a few sessions with the traditional literature circle model, as detailed in the previous chapter, we drop the roles (if we use them at all) and move to more free-form, student-driven discussions—similar to a book group that I would engage in as an adult. When I attend book club meetings at the university or with personal friends, I'm not required to complete work in advance, and I respect that students can intelligently discuss their way through a novel in a group setting without this kind of preparatory work. Please see Chapter 3 for an extensive discussion on the formation and development of book groups and ideas for supporting student discussions.

Example: Collaborative Topic Videos

At the end of the first marking period at my school, after students have completed the shared text (and often others) and extensively discussed the topics (domains) associated with the texts, they consider how they want to contribute to the world via their *practice*, which will serve as their summative assessments. I prefer that students select their own modes of practice. Often, we work together as a class to determine how they want to engage in this practice, and then students go back to their groups to work collaboratively and define individual responsibilities. As a steward, I share ideas if students need support, but I encourage them to draft out a list of project needs and utilize their strengths. One particularly popular form of practice is the creation of videos, in which students share their reading and thinking publicly.

When videos are an item of interest, I show the students professional book trailers, and we analyze the strengths and weaknesses of each. I invite students to be critical consumers by considering what they feel is missing from the videos. To inspire new reading ideas, I intentionally share trailers of books that I have in my classroom and that can be found in the library. We also explore YouTube together to identify student-generated topic videos. One video that a group of students found to be particularly inspiring to their own work was the "Drop the I-Word" campaign video (www.raceforward.org/practice/tools/drop-i-word). When my first group of students engaged in the creation of videos, they chose to share about their books by creating book trailers. Across the semesters of teaching the course, however, other communities of practice felt that this engagement in book trailers wasn't contributing enough to their community and the world. They suggested we use the books as a jumping-off point, so often the book was only a small slice of the video, which was more focused on the topic or message inspired by the book that the students wanted to share with the world.

To begin, students selected one of the especially inspiring titles they read as a group, something that compelled them to act with agency. Then they co-created a video designed to share their learning about the topic; the video also served to share more about the book that inspired their thinking. Groups that focused a bit more on the book were able to think about literary concepts such as themes, author's craft, and mood. One group of students, for example, selected clips of both classical and rock music to express the main character's disparate feelings toward the two school systems in the novel, and they then shared messages about inequities they themselves saw across school systems beyond the book. Another student, who chose to work independently and had experience with video editing, challenged herself and learned how to integrate concepts from video games to establish the mood of a thriller that her group had read, and she then considered how she could share her video publicly with the gaming world. There are several standard and free movie applications, such as iMovie, that are user-friendly for students.

In my classroom, we had only one computer, so students rotated using the computer during the week to ensure access for all. But the videos were just one option of a summative assessment that my community of practice co-designed, and other groups developed other ideas for analyzing their texts and collaborating on outward-facing forms of practice. Sharing past students' videos seemed to consistently inspire students to want to create their own videos, and this also built an increasingly long to-be-read list of books because of the powerful ways the books appeared in these videos.

Independent Reading

In the previous chapter, I briefly outlined an independent reading program in existing courses, but here I offer a more detailed exploration of what this might look like in a stand-alone course and how we might assess student progress. We can decentralize ourselves in classrooms and act as stewards, yet as teachers we are usually expected to fill in a gradebook at the end of each semester. Independent reading is an aspect of instruction that teachers identify as being particularly difficult to assess.

I believe without question that it's crucial for students to read *during* class. I have never worked with a student-based community of practice that disagreed with this belief. Many of my students chose to enroll in my course because this was the only time they had to read amid their busy lives. What we as teachers value is reflected in how we use our available time in school, so we must as stewards work to develop this time and space in our classrooms. If we claim to value reading, that task shouldn't be relegated to home but instead included as a central element of our daily schedule. If students never have the opportunity to read in school, they might infer that reading isn't as important as other class activities that we value in schools like, say, test prep. Models such as sustained silent reading (SSR), drop everything and read (DEAR), and free uninterrupted reading (FUR) are vital for students of all ages. It's clear that "free reading is the source of our reading prowess and much of our vocabulary and spelling development, as well as our ability to understand sophisticated phrases and write coherent prose" (Krashen, 2006, p. 43).

If your community of practice agrees to employ silent reading methods, I encourage you to agree to do so fully, allotting significant time for students to settle in and immerse themselves in the stories they've chosen. The desired amount of independent reading time will vary across communities of practice, but most often, the communities I have worked with have chosen to start with around twenty-five minutes of silent reading, and then we check in with our community to determine whether this amount of time is appropriate. In the following sections, I offer ways you might assess and evaluate independent reading.

Reading Conferences

Providing students time to read in class allows you, as steward and as a person accountable to a school system through a gradebook, to gather necessary information on student progress. I host two types of conferences—teacher conferences and peer/community conferences. As the students read, you might sit and conference quietly with individual students to check in, assess understanding, and solicit concerns. Assessing independent reading requires planning and flexibility. Unlike shared whole-class texts, students are working at their own individualized paces.

This is something that I celebrate rather than fear. You might work with students independently during their reading conferences to track their progress, check comprehension, praise their efforts, recommend books that might come next on a reading ladder (Lesesne, 2010) that will challenge them (intellectually, rather than in terms of reading level), and just sit in the joy of reading. Lesesne's philosophy asks students to build a ladder as they read in order to continually challenge their thinking. This might involve choosing a more thematically complex text or exploring a topic in a text in a different genre. I usually start a reading conference by jotting down what the student is reading and what they've read since our last conference. Then I pose the open-ended statement, "Talk to me about your reading." This allows the student to guide the conference. Some students need more prodding, and a few questions that guide our conversations are:

- How are you doing as a reader? What are you doing well as a reader? What are you struggling with as a reader?
- Are there parts of the text that are or were confusing to you?
- How would you like to improve as a reader? How can I support you?
- What can you tell me about your book? What questions do you have about your book? What do you find challenging about your book?
- What is your general appraisal of this title? Would you recommend it to others? Why or why not?
- What does the author of this title do well? What would you recommend they do differently?
- What are your next steps?

These questions serve as a guide, and communities of practice that are accustomed to reading conferences can even build these questions together. Following the conference, I jot notes to myself about the conference in general, areas that the student is focusing on improving, and ways I can support the student or ask a peer to offer the student support. At two points during the semester, students self-evaluate their progress in relation to their goals. We do this together during a reading conference. Some aspects they have chosen to consider in their self-evaluations are:

- Sharing the texts they are reading with others (during our daily book talks)
- Making progress toward reading goals (set during our first conference and revised throughout)
- Stretching their abilities (trying on new genres/forms, challenging themselves with books they perceive to be complex, increasing reading stamina, etc.)

I've taught the course for many semesters, and I have always agreed with students' self-evaluations. That said, you could easily co-generate a rubric with students rather than using this holistic approach.

You can regularly conference with students about their goals and the texts they are currently reading. Although we want our students to be immersed in as many books as possible, it's important to assess their understanding of the texts they read. Encouraging them to increase the volume and variety of texts they access doesn't ensure that they are comprehending their reading. One formative assessment method that communities of practice have selected is to monitor comprehension using sticky notes. As students read, they can place sticky notes on pages to mark important passages or questions to discuss with their peers and you. Conferences with students and these sticky notes allow for an assessment of students' reading comprehension without undermining their joy in reading. When students finish texts, you can ask them to transfer their sticky notes to a piece of paper to hold in a reading portfolio.

After I have held a few conferences with students, the entire community of practice checks in to discuss the conferencing process. Most students have never had a conference focused solely on their reading, but they are accustomed to writing conferences. Together we revise the process of the reading conference format to work for them and their goals related to both their reading and their domain(s). Then I elevate the reading conferences by asking students to conduct *peer* conferences. Sometimes students select a peer who has read the same book or shares a similar domain (if the domains are independent). This is another way that I work to decentralize myself in the community of practice while still allowing for spaces where students are being supported in their independent reading and learning. I work to ensure that all of my students feel supported, and I also rely on peers within the community of practice to offer that same support.

Over the years, students have expressed that they like to keep track of their reading in some way—adding books they've read to a Goodreads shelf, making a list or writing titles in their binder or notebook for the class, etc. I don't ever force students to complete reading logs because I think logs and tracking can suck the fun out of reading. I am aware of critics who agree that this is a form of extrinsic rather than intrinsic motivation. Yet my students request it and enjoy doing it, so it's optional for them. As an adult, I don't want to write down how many pages I read each day, so I allow students to work together to develop a tracking system (if this is an interest) that supports them in sharing how they are meeting reading goals and/or sharing the books they've finished. Most choose to write the titles of books they finish on a page in their notebooks, but others have been more creative in their display of the titles. One semester, students chose to create posters with large thermometers showing their reading goals and book titles. Another year, in which the students took different approaches to tracking their progress, a student wrote the titles on the side of her shoe. She said, "I carry my books with me everywhere, and they help me move forward in life."

Independent Reading Mini-Projects and Reading Portfolios

When you finish a book at home, I'd bet that the last thing you want to do is write a book report. If you made me write a book report for the book I am reading right now, I wouldn't finish the book! I encourage communities of practice not only to develop a way to evaluate their comprehension (e.g., sticky notes and teacher or peer reading conferences), but also to create an ongoing assessment, or practice, that is quite different from a book report but that allows them to share their cumulative reading across the semester in an outward-facing way.

In my class, there is an element of the community of practice that lives on across semesters: the reading portfolio. I have never had a group of students choose a different practice once they see what other students in previous classes have done. This is a method that I did as a college student in Wendy Glenn's young adult literature class, and it lives on more than a decade later with my own students. The students complete one-pagers (one single-sided page of a standard piece of paper) to demonstrate their overall understanding of their independently read books. This project offers a lot of freedom. Each one-pager creatively demonstrates their reading in some way. For instance, one student who read *The Astonishing Color of After* by Emily X. R. Pan (2018) wrote a funeral notice, and another student wrote a musical number to be performed for the community within Cynthia Leitich Smith's *Hearts Unbroken* (2020). These one-pagers, as a formative assessment, give students a finite structure in which to frame their product, and it reduces the paper load. Additionally, these projects allow students to focus on the joy of reading, which the aforementioned dreaded book report tends to squash. It's important to provide students with choices for their one-pagers, as different books lend themselves to different approaches.

Over the years, I have collected some one-pager exemplars and kept them in a binder that rests atop my classroom library. When students struggle to find a book, they peruse the binder for books that other students have loved. This practice also becomes more outward-facing when students take the binders to events such as our book fair, community read-ins, and elective choice nights (when students learn about the school electives before course scheduling). Sample project options have included the following: (1) design a social media page for one of the characters in your book, (2) write a letter to the Board of Education arguing for your book to be incorporated into the curriculum, (3) take and share a collection of photographs inspired by your book, or (4) design a social event that a character from your book might attend. Communities of practice design their own forms of practice, yet the reputation of this project and the idea that their one-pagers can be donated to live on for future students often proves irresistible. Together students can brainstorm a list of one-pager options that would meet the expectations of an assignment. This encourages them to think creatively and expansively when they work on their one-pagers.

These one-pagers then become part of the larger reading portfolio assignment, which students self-assess for a grade in the gradebook (if you have a pesky gradebook that requires numbers, like I had). If the students are writing sticky notes for comprehension as they read, I also encourage them to transfer these from their books. The sticky notes (or other form of comprehension), along with the one-pagers, constitute one part of the portfolio. The students also find other ways to demonstrate self-reflection on their reading growth to be shared in the portfolio. Some semesters this is a written reflection. One semester, students asked to write "literacy histories and literacy futures." The reading portfolio isn't mandatory and is just one way that a community of practice might evaluate their independent reading across a semester. I have found that students experience joy and pride in looking at a portfolio of their reading across the year.

Another mini-project that students might use for independent reading is Carrie Melnychenko's Character File Analysis Project (see the following vignette). Using a standard file folder, students analyze the characters in their independent reading texts. This project allows students to celebrate their reading around the room and asks them to critically analyze the characters in the books they read and to share their work with peers.

The Character File Analysis Project

Carrie Melnychenko
Huron High School, New Boston, MI
Email: melnychenko@sbcglobal.net

When my co-teacher, students, and I designed our school's first ever YA literature course, we put in tons of time reading, attempting to select the perfect novels for students. Because this class had to include analytical writing, just like other, more traditional English classes, we quickly realized that the writing needed to go beyond the standard five-paragraph essay or the traditional book report. Students needed to be excited about the writing as well as the books they were reading.

We asked students what kinds of analysis they wanted to do. How could they write about their reading in a nontraditional way? How could we open the door to creativity? Could the analysis be interactive with other students? Their response became the Character File Analysis Project.

Students use a standard file folder, which they decorate in any way that makes sense with the independent novel they have just finished reading. The front cover shows an image of the author and/or book as well as a brief biography. The back cover includes three book reviews from different sources. Inside is the analysis. Together, we decided to include (in paragraph form):

- A physical and personality description of the protagonist(s)
- A description of what motivates this character's actions
- Detailed descriptions of various types of conflict
- If and how the conflict was resolved
- One possible theme
- A comparison of the protagonist to a historical or modern-day figure
- Creative images, whether student-created or found on the internet, strewn throughout the interior of the folder

(See Figure 4.2 for a picture of the folders on display on our bulletin board!)

Figure 4.2. Character File Analysis Projects on the wall of my classroom.

We loved reading these character profiles, and we loved displaying them in the classroom for other students to see. Over the years, students who in years prior I had to really push to write even a short paper produced in-depth analysis and creative flair. Because they weren't bound to the traditional thesis-statement-and-three-more-paragraphs kind of writing, they opened up and decided what they wanted to value in their character files.

Engaging Students in Passion Projects and Connection

The whole-class, small-group, and individual learning experiences that I described in the previous section shift and move with the community of practice's needs and interests. Every semester, the students drive the content of the course and how this is organized within intentional co-planning sessions. The structure feels experimental every semester because the students co-generate a course that will be most fulfilling, rewarding, and challenging for them. There are course experiences that I have shared from past semesters (like the reading portfolio) which have remained fairly consistent across semesters. They move beyond the whole-class, small group, and individual structures. Students always, in some form, engage in choice passion projects—independently, in small groups, or as a whole class—and I always ensure that our work throughout the entire semester is engaged with the community virtually, physically, and globally. Below, I describe what these might look like as learning experiences and how these became forms of *practice*.

Choice Passion Projects

In the second half of the course, I encourage students to design and develop passion projects on some aspect of interest related to young adult literature. Modeled around the freedom inherent in Juliani's (2014) conception of Genius Hour, I encourage students to find a project that they will love doing—something that will bring them joy and enrichment as they explore a domain of interest. This is where many of the students connect deeply with the community of practice, and they often discover overlapping interests. The community works together to explore what they are each passionate about—topics and themes (domains)—relevant to the local community and/or global needs. One set of students developed a community-wide literacy event, and another group invited members of the community into our classroom for their project. Whatever the project, they focus intensely on engagement (with their community or globally) as they develop their *practice*. They design projects connected to their interests and with specific purposes. I remind students that their independent choice books can be read through the lens of their passion project. In other words, if a student wants to write a book-in-verse about mental health to share with students at the local middle school, that student should probably read at least one middle grade book-in-verse while thinking about their project goals.

These passion projects require heavy conferencing (both teacher and peer) because most students are overwhelmed with the freedom of the project. Year after year, the vast majority of students change their project idea at least once after hearing about their classmates' projects and after sitting with and trying out their ideas. The project products vary widely, but all students are required to share their ideas with the community of practice to invite feedback and also to share, following the conclusion of the projects, their learning processes with our community. This allows them to share their passions while developing their oral language and public speaking skills. (It also allows me to meet a school standard in the gradebook.)

The concept of the passion project is one I have developed with both high school and college student communities of practice, and I have found the caliber of the projects to be high, regardless of the age level of the students. Here are some of the projects that students have developed:

- Slam poetry performed at a student-developed evening open mic event
- A song inspired by Jandy Nelson's *I'll Give You the Sun* (2015), which the student wrote, recorded (www.youtube.com/watch?v=We5bQfbSfz4), and performed live
- A dance inspired by Jason Reynolds's *Long Way Down* (2017) that was choreographed, recorded (www.youtube.com/watch?v=vsrGh3QQKYY), and performed live using the audiobook as the music
- A choose-your-own adventure YA novel that was then shared at a bookstore event
- A YA pop-up book designed with an artist in the local community
- A video game inspired by a text and played with youth at a boys and girls club
- The development of a linguistic economics system that can be used to analyze any YA text (designed with a local professor)
- A study of the linguistic contexts of YA texts and engagement with the community to host a brown bag luncheon to discuss linguistic context
- A manuscript co-written with me for scholarly publication to analyze a domain

The projects that emerge from this end-of-year assessment are rewarding for our entire community of practice. We co-design their end-of-semester presentations, but students often begin their presentations by sharing the books that inspired or guided their work. This provides more reading ideas for students to consider before the course ends. The project presentation day is quite magical as we witness the many ways YA literature can be incorporated into our work and lives and hear about student experiences doing work in the community.

In the opening of this chapter, I described a shared, whole-class passion project in which we took a trip to a bookstore, and students worked in groups with shared passions around specific interests. Passion projects need not be independent; the entire class can engage in shared questions and explorations together.

Virtual and Community Connections

The field of YA literature has a powerful place virtually. Many authors forge strong connections with their readers through social media. On several occasions, my class has tweeted a question to an author, and the author responded. Further, readers of YA literature are connected across social media (see Chapter 5 for a more detailed discussion), which provides readers a space to read loudly and to engage in conversation about the literature. For this reason, your community of practice might talk about virtual connections in your co-generated course design. During class we look at how authors choose to promote their work and connect with audiences.

Over the duration of the course, students can participate on Goodreads (www.goodreads.com), which, as mentioned previously, is a social networking website that allows students to post book reviews and discuss book-related topics online. This website exposes students to hundreds of millions of books and encourages them to network with other readers who share their interests. If your community of practice chooses to engage with Goodreads, as steward you can secure student profiles and create discussion groups that aren't visible to the public (if needed). To be on the safe side, you might also ask parents, guardians, and caregivers to peruse the website and sign off on letting their children participate. Earlier in the chapter, I noted that my students review books on Goodreads, but it can also be used by your community of practice to host an online discussion group and examine crowd-sourced lists. Students can post on a range of topics. Many choose to use Goodreads to track their books and set reading goals.

Every semester at least one student in my class chooses a passion project that spreads the love of reading in outward-facing, public ways. Students have reached out to other teachers in the school and our middle school to give five-minute book talks about recently published good books to their peers. Students have also reached out to the local bookstore and public library to give book talks in the children's section. One semester a pair of students who wanted to become elementary school teachers connected with the local elementary schools to read with students and share picture book suggestions. These passion projects spread the love of reading and allow the students to read loudly.

In her YA literature class, Brooke Bianchi-Pennington (featured in a previous vignette) works with students to host their school's reading blog, which they name *HVA [Hardin Valley Academy] Reads*. This blog demonstrates how the four walls of the classroom can be extended in extraordinary ways. Brooke's students form six committees to host the blog and connect with the community:

- Web Design and Upkeep: Students who are web-design savvy control the layout and pages of the website and post student work.

- Social Media Managers: Students who manage social media promotion of the blog and share general news related to literacy and YA literature.
- Physical Project Developers: Students who promote the blog physically within the school (fliers, bulletin boards, book carts, library displays).
- Editors: Students who develop guidelines for each post and examine them for language and appropriateness.
- Community Outreach/Literary Agents: Students who reach out to the community to promote the blog and literacy. They reach out to authors/guest speakers, schedule library events, and work with local bookstores and other classes.
- Content Creators: Although each student will submit posts to the blog, this committee is tasked with posting additional content at least once a week.

Brooke's community of practice demonstrates the real ways in which teachers situate their courses in authentic experiences and allow students to work collaboratively to spread the love of reading. The students work together to submit to the NPR Student Podcast Challenge each semester around a shared topic, such as censorship in YA literature.

Logistical Concerns with Creating a New Course

With the approval of a stand-alone course comes incredible excitement—and the potentially unnerving reality of countless possibilities for course design! Prior to this, you and your colleagues may face many logistical concerns, such as acquiring the necessary books and other materials, soliciting students for the course, setting up the classroom space and classroom library effectively, and designing course curricula. You may know you want to create a co-generated community of practice, but as steward, you need help before you reach this point. There are numerous ways to approach and tackle these challenges; the suggestions in this section reflect my lived experiences and may provide helpful, albeit not singular, solutions.

Introducing and Justifying the Idea

Even if you are passionate about young adult literature, you may encounter resistance from colleagues and leaders within the school community. People are often quick to misjudge the value of YA literature, assuming it to be of lesser quality than canonical texts and including potentially inappropriate content, rendering it unworthy of inclusion in the classroom. To demonstrate the necessity of the course, you might show teachers and administrators the power and merit of these texts (see Chapter 1). One way to increase buy-in is to recommend books to individuals in the school and community that are tailored to their reading interests. Another is to draw on the expertise of students in our advocacy efforts. The most compelling way to justify the value of the course is to build a network of readers willing and able to attest to the important role books play in their lives as young people. Students should be encouraged to read loudly. When impacted by a powerful story, they should share it with both their peers and the adults in their lives in and out of school. They should feel empowered to take control of their educational experience by soliciting time dedicated to reading and sharing texts in the classroom setting. When it's the students who are calling for additional time to access these books, administrators, colleagues, and school board members are more likely to approve a course to accommodate this request.

Drafting a Proposal

I quickly and happily discovered that the course proposal process wasn't nearly as daunting and unfriendly as I had imagined. As a useful reference, I offer a sample course proposal in Figure 4.3. Such a document would probably be submitted to school and/or district administrators, curriculum coordinators, and the Board of Education. It's written with care to address reading and writing skills and standardized tests (the currency of many Boards of Education). To garner the support of these groups, you might want to address how the course will enhance students' reading skills and likely improve results on state assessments taken in their required English language arts courses. When advocating for the course, it's essential to clarify that a stand-alone YA literature class should not be a remedial or intervention course; all students should be encouraged to enroll, as course content is differentiated based on student needs. As stressed in Chapter 1, YA literature has value equivalent to canonical titles, and interesting, relevant texts should be offered to students at all levels. When seeking course approval, you should be prepared to justify the value of YA literature and be primed to answer questions about censorship (see Chapter 3).

Acquiring Necessary Books and Other Materials

To avoid extensive out-of-pocket costs, you might acquire books and other materials from the generous financial support of others. Below I describe a few of my favorite donation and revenue sources:

NCTE Annual Convention
In November of each year, the National Council of Teachers of English (NCTE) (ncte.org) sponsors an annual convention. Representatives from major publishing houses attend this event and set up tables in the Exhibit Hall. In addition to selling books at discounted rates, publishers provide attendees opportunities to acquire advanced reader copies of new young adult books to

Figure 4.3. One example of a proposal for a new YA literature elective. Please keep in mind the audience for this proposal, which influenced my stress on aspects like standardized testing.

New Course Proposal: Young Adult Literature Elective

1. Name and Description of the Course

Young Adult Literature will provide the opportunity for committed students to enhance their reading skills with contemporary literature. All of the reading for this course will be co-generated and interest-based. Most texts will be selected from award-winning, bestselling, and quick pick lists. The course is designed to hone students' reading skills and develop their understanding of trends and marketing in literature today. They will examine contemporary writing and consider how current literature is analyzed and critiqued today. As students study the literature, they will work to co-develop the course design. We will use a readers' and writers' workshop model, where they will work to improve their reading and writing skills by writing in a variety of styles. They will be taught to understand and value the importance of revision using state test editing strategies. Students will also be exposed to reading skills used in the reading comprehension section of the SAT test. The major focus of this class is to encourage students to become more critical readers and contemporary writers while introducing them to the many trends and styles of the literature of today. This course is grounded in the objective of motivating students at all levels to read, to read widely, and to read with many purposes. Their projects will engage with local and global audiences.

2. Length of Course, Frequency of Meetings, and Credits

Young Adult Literature will be a one-semester, half-credit elective English course open to all students in grades 10–12.

3. Topical Outline of the Course

Students will read contemporary texts of different styles and respond based on the strategies that can be used for the state test. Students will work together to define topics of interest for engaging with local and global issues and will use a readers' and writers' workshop model to enhance their revision and peer-editing techniques. This course is designed to prepare our students to be critical and to engage with community both inside and outside of the classroom. Literary assessments will be developed based on the readings and skills taught. The assessment of student writing will be rubric-based with student input on the construction of the rubrics.

4. Goals and Objectives of the Course

- Students will learn and study current trends and styles in contemporary literature.
- Students will model writing styles and write for public audiences.
- Students will engage in wide reading and become more critical readers and contemporary writers.
- Students will co-generate practices for engaging with local and global audiences.

5. Reason for Addition

This elective course is designed to improve student test scores by focusing on reading skills and writing techniques. The vast amount of (supported) reading the student will engage with will work toward improving their reading comprehension skills, and the focus on critical writing will aid students in enhancing their writing test scores. There is presently no course available for students who wish to study contemporary and/or young adult literature. There has been a large demand from students to read recently written texts, and this course will allow students to dive deeply into rich understandings of aspects such as the marketing, publication, and critique of current, contemporary texts while enhancing their test scores.

6. Vertical and Horizontal Relation to Other Courses

Many students select contemporary texts during the independent reading portion of our tenth-grade curriculum. This course will help hone their reading skills and guide them to better understand what they read.

7. Estimated Cost of Implementing This Course

Resource Texts: $500 (for the purchase of trade books)

8. Implications on Staffing

None

9. Pilot Testing Recommended

2010–2011 school year

10. Proposal Developed by

Ricki Ginsberg

11. Date of Implementation

September 2010 (Note: I have adapted the course proposal slightly from the original version.)

12. Signatures

Department Head ______________________ Date ______________
Coordinator ______________________ Date ______________
Principal ______________________ Date ______________

Course Description for the Student Handbook:

Young Adult Literature Fall/Spring Semester Credit: 0.50

Prerequisites: This course is open to students in grades 10, 11, and 12.

Description: This one-semester course is devoted to the study of young adult literature with an emphasis on contemporary local and global issues. All of the reading and assignments for this course will be interest-based, and the course will be individualized to student needs and also developed in community.

be published later in the year. These books are free to teacher and librarian attendees and provide us a way to peruse upcoming titles we might wish to introduce to students. My students feel great joy at the opportunity to sample these titles as well. Rather than taking books at random, I have found it to be more useful to speak with the publishing representatives about my students and their interests and needs. They can tailor suggestions in ways that are much more beneficial than I can if I'm grabbing books at random. Free posters and book swag that can be used to excite students are also abundant at the NCTE Convention. Publishing companies often provide posters advertising their newest books that can occupy the empty space on our classroom walls.

ALAN Workshop

The Assembly on Literature for Adolescents of the National Council of Teachers of English (ALAN) (alan-ya.org) holds its annual workshop the Monday and Tuesday immediately following the NCTE Convention. This nonprofit organization is devoted solely to the promotion of young adult literature. Workshop attendees are provided a free one-year membership to the organization; this includes a subscription to the journal, *The ALAN Review*. Each year, recently published and well-known YA authors attend this workshop and speak about their writing. Attendees receive a large box of new books, are invited to speak with and learn from the authors at events, and, through breakout sessions and social gatherings, are encouraged to network with other educators, librarians, authors, and publishers in the field. The organization hosts a Facebook page and group, Instagram account, and Twitter account that allow teachers, librarians, publishers, and authors to connect and share ideas related to YA literature.

School Funding via Textbook Budgets

You may be fortunate enough to have earmarked departmental or school funds with textbook budgets to purchase books for the new class. In the course proposal, it may be wise to request a small amount of funding to acquire an initial set of books from which a larger collection can be built. I operate under the belief that it never hurts to ask if a small budget would be possible to promote reading in the school!

School Library Budgets

School libraries may be able to budget for and accommodate requests for a class that is focused on the promotion of reading. While librarians are not likely to fund an entire classroom set (which, given the choice component of the elective course, isn't necessary anyway), they may be able to purchase sets of four to six copies of popular titles. Additionally, some libraries are able to acquire small sets of books from other facilities in their region.

Grants

If the school can't provide funding for books and other materials, you (and students!) could apply for local and national grants. For instance, each year you can apply to the ALAN Foundation Grant for up to $1,500 if you want to do research centered on some element of YA literature in your classroom (www .alan-ya.org/awards/alan-foundation-grant). As a classroom teacher, I applied for this grant and received a computer that I used to implement new virtual connections in my YA literature course. You might also apply for grants sponsored by organizations like DonorsChoose.org, an online charity dedicated to helping classrooms in need.

Donations

Local businesses sometimes donate money to purchase books for classrooms in their community. With the school's permission, you might help students organize a collection effort. To reward participating businesses, you could create a donor poster for public distribution or include donor names on stickers placed on the inside covers of the books purchased. Additionally, students could develop their critical reviewing skills as they determine which books to add to the classroom library and engage in meaningful writing practices by drafting thank-you notes to participating businesses.

Publisher-Sponsored Book Fairs

Book fairs are not just for elementary or middle school children; Scholastic Publishing, for example, willingly accepts requests from and accommodates high school communities. The fairs are easy to manage and can be opened to the public. With one weeklong book fair and a lot of signs around my city, my YA literature elective students, for instance, earned more than one thousand dollars in rewards to be spent on new books. Students are able to work as volunteers, and English teachers can bring their classes to explore. Scholastic also holds warehouse sales around the country that offer educators and book fair volunteers affordable discounts on hundreds of books.

School Activities

Another way to generate revenue for course materials—and interest in the course—is through student fundraising activities. You might consider managing events such as plays, ice cream socials, volleyball lock-ins, or movie nights in a school location to generate hundreds of dollars for new books.

Soliciting Students for the Course

The best way to solicit students for the course is by word of mouth. In the first year of implementation, you may depend on former students enrolled in their regular English classes to spread the word. Colleagues and guidance counselors can also prove invaluable in recommending the course to students. If you are sponsoring a book fair, you might recruit volunteers and ask them to discuss the class with every student who walks into the book fair. Posters can be strategically placed around the school, and fliers can be distributed to students in their English classes.

Recruiting efforts in the second year of the course will likely prove easier, as students in the first year might stage read-ins, create videos to be shown in other classes, or set up an informational table during lunch times. Word of mouth and the public nature of students' passion projects also tend to generate more enrollment in the course. You might also ask other teachers if the Young Adult Literature course students could share book recommendations with their students and simultaneously share about the elective.

When marketing the course, be sure the course description is worded in a way that will interest and excite students. Students should get the impression that the class provides a comfortable space and place to read and share books with their peers while learning more about topics they are interested in exploring. Rather than asking students if they like to read, ask them if they have ever enjoyed reading. Unfortunately, many middle and high schoolers don't enjoy reading or don't attach joy to reading in school, but they remember a time in their childhoods or earlier schooling when they found reading to be interesting and exciting (see Chapter 1). Students should understand that this stand-alone course is devoted to the (re)development of that passion.

Setting Up the Classroom

Colorful, student-centered classrooms allow students to see the classroom space as inviting, interactive, and comfortable. Posters about reading and displays of student work and community engagement that emerge from reading activities create an atmosphere that encourages students to learn about and share a love of literature. Comfortable couches, beanbags, and flexible seating provide relaxing sitting areas that serve as alternatives to traditional, and often confining, desks.

To invite students to explore titles independently, you and your students might strategically place books throughout the classroom with care and intention. If students choose to write recommendations about favorite books, these can be posted on brightly colored paper around the classroom. If you run out of wall space, book posters and recommendations can be strategically placed by students around the school—even on the back of bathroom stalls! It's important to surround the community of practice with titles so they are never at a loss for potential reading material.

Some of my students enjoyed public expressions of their reading and have centered this in their community of practice. While I always let students know that I value the intrinsic rather than the extrinsic love of reading, if the community of practice wants to flaunt their love of reading to others, I take a step back and watch. Sometimes they create wall space dedicated to their love of reading for others to see. One year the class decided to host a massive competition with the other section of the elective. One drawback of reading competitions (as with reading logs, as shared previously) is that they can downplay the intrinsic rewards that students experience when they finish enjoyable books. Similarly, as a parent I agonize about our district library's competition each year. I want my children to read for the sake of reading rather than to earn prizes. So I reminded students that we don't want to attach pressure to the competition across sections, but I found that the competition simply added another layer of excitement for students—and it was their idea. They weren't reading *for* the competition; instead, it was another way for them to celebrate and share their love of books with others.

Students walked into the room and immediately approached their wall of books, giggling as they saw their score increase as peers added new books they wanted others to read. The competition was easy and hands-off for me, as the students documented the pages of their completed books on a class poster (drawing stars next to their favorites, of course) and added the number of pages in the book to the team total. As a bonus, students were able to see all of the books their peers were reading, which enabled them to discover peers who were reading the same texts and discuss the books with members of the class or across sections. It also gave them a go-to list of texts when they were in search of new titles. So although I'm not a big fan of reading competitions and agree with colleagues who speak out against them for the reasons noted, I was a member of the community of practice, the competition was their idea, and it was an idea that excited them during their community brainstorming session. I used some of my leftover funds to buy bulk sets of bookmarks to give to each student at the end of the semester. Everyone loved reading, so everyone won.

Setting Up the Classroom Library

Keeping track of books in your classroom library can be difficult. You might use a clipboard, but when a lot of students are signing out books, this can become unnecessarily messy and complicated. To make the process more manageable and encourage greater student autonomy, library cards and pockets can be purchased inexpensively online. Using this system, students sign out books and leave the cards in a box; when they're finished with the texts, they sign them back in on their own. You can organize the system so that you aren't involved in the library checkout process at all. Alternatively, there are easy-to-manage digital systems for keeping track of collections. As a high school teacher and now a college professor, I have used Booksource Classroom (booksource.com/content/Booksource-Classroom.aspx) as a library management tool and found it worked well. Even better, you could invite your students to help you co-organize the library during a study hall period.

To make the books themselves more visually appealing and likely to be checked out, you might display the newest or most popular books on the tops of shelves and cabinets; students have told me that this is where they look first when selecting titles. Within the shelves, students might find it useful to divide books by genre so they can see other books similar to titles that they've read and enjoyed. But sorting by genre can also prevent students from expanding their reading repertoire, and some books may be difficult to sort into a single genre; you can remedy this in a classroom discussion with explicit attention to these limitations and by moving books across genres often. And, of course, one of the most effective ways to promote titles is to create a shifting "student favorites" shelf that celebrates the books students love most. In the following vignette, teacher-librarian Kellee Moye offers more tips for and perspective on acquiring books, conceptualizing and organizing the classroom library, and surveying students.

Example of Creating a Classroom Library: The Heart of a Literacy Classroom

Kellee Moye
Hunter's Creek Middle School, Orlando, Florida
Twitter: @kelleemoye @unleashreaders
Facebook: Unleashing Readers

Having a classroom library is more than just providing access to books. It's about showing how important books and reading are to you and your students. Just by having shelves filled with books in your classroom, you are sending a message to your students that books are a priority to you and your students. My classroom library is a point of pride and joy for my students and me. My library started with three shelves on a bookshelf in 2006 and has grown to approximately 4,000 titles.

Many people ask how I get so many books on a teacher's salary, and my biggest hints are:

- Use Book Orders to earn points to get free books.
- Take donations.
- Visit Goodwill and used bookstores.
- Have an Amazon wish list with the titles you want.
- Partner with DonorsChoose.

With these and time you will plant and cultivate a beautiful classroom library. See Figure 4.4 for a picture of my library.

Figure 4.4. My classroom library.

As for organizing the classroom library, I have tried a couple of different ways, but what my students and I have found works best is a mixture. Fiction is in alphabetical order by author's last name, just as in the school and public libraries. This allows students looking for a specific author to easily find them. We also sticker my books with colored dots to show the genre. We sticker for four main fiction genres: realistic fiction, science fiction, fantasy, and historical fiction. We also sticker three formats: graphic novel, poetry, and short story. These stickers help students looking for a certain type of book find them easily.

Our nonfiction we separate into sections: informational nonfiction, narrative nonfiction, biography, traditional literature (e.g., myths), and poetry collections. Each of these sections is organized differently. Biography books (with memoirs and autobiographies) are alphabetized by the subject's last name, informational and narrative nonfiction is separated into topics, traditional literature is organized by place of origin, and poetry is alphabetical by poet. They are all stickered to match their genre and are given a format sticker if it fits.

We do also have a popular series section to make these books easier to find, and we separate out the graphic novels because of their popularity. Last, we have quite a few baskets where students put books that they rated five stars. This allows students to see what others have loved.

And the last step of having a classroom library is setting policy and procedures. I include a letter in my syllabus that tells families I have a large range of books in my classroom library and there is no way for me to know what they would find appropriate for their child, so I do not stop students from checking out books they're interested in; however, if they don't want their child to read a particular book, to please let me know. Thanks to this letter, I have had no complaints or censorship issues [see Chapter 3 for more strategies for dealing with censorship]. I then allow students to check out up to two books at a time for as long as they need to finish. (During school breaks, I do allow students to go "shopping" and take home as many books as they want!)

Once the students understand and have approved the classroom library procedures and policies, they can enjoy the books! I always remind myself: having the classroom library is step one; allowing students choice of books and time to read are steps 2 and 3. As my student Carlos wrote to me, "The best thing about your class and the library was that you gave us choices. The choice to read, the choice to succeed, and the choice to fail. Since you were really the first teacher to give me those choices I decided to take them. It was when I had you that I actually started reading for fun. School in general was never presented to me as a choice but rather as an absolute and you completely shattered that and I thank you for that."

More responses to "Are Classroom Libraries Beneficial?" are available at www.unleashingreaders.com/?p=10632 along with any of my blog posts about my end-of-year survey.

Conclusion

A driving force behind my Young Adult Literature course was my desire to co-generate a place and space that allowed students critical freedom to shape the course objectives and offer their own critique on domains, or topics of interest. Included in this mission was a desire for us to expand our knowledge of different titles and read often, read widely, and read loudly. This course overwhelms students and me with the sheer number of domains for exploration and quality texts available for engaging in locally and globally connected practice. Students have described the ways they felt a stand-alone course liberated them from inflexible curricular structures and allowed them to develop practices that were authentic and engaged. Some readers who enrolled in one section of the course described how they were supported in deconstructing their experiences in traditional classroom spaces, building new conceptions of themselves as readers, and shaping their individual reading identities with agency (Glenn & Ginsberg, 2016). Teachers of stand-alone young adult literature courses are often able to co-generate course design more freely with students. They can focus with students more acutely on co-designing forms of practice that will allow the students to be stronger, more effective readers, to nourish and spread a love of reading, and to engage as critically conscious and involved community members—all factors that will catapult their growth in aspects of more traditional schooling and on standardized assessments. Students recommend books to one another daily, explore new titles, share book ideas, and critique and contribute to the field. They participate thoughtfully in their communities of practice and find opportunities to engage locally and globally.

Chapter Five

Leading Literate Lives Together

The powerful potential of young adult literature encourages communities of practice to look inward at ourselves as readers—our practices, our connections to reading, our histories of reading. Yet I feature it so strongly in this text for the ways it allows us to forge connections with the world—with other readers and thinkers, scholars, authors, students, and communities. These connections are binding and lasting, offering us the grand, fulfilling ability to lead literate lives ourselves—and the gift of working alongside students as they do the same. The possibilities are vast for both us and our students.

In this chapter, I invite you to first think about how our communities of practice can better know the literature and be readers. Both of these principles—knowing the literature and being a reader—are really stances toward YA literature as well as stances toward teaching: when we lead a readerly life, we can discover the joy that comes from reading strong texts about young adults, a joy we can share with our students. We can also become thoughtful recommenders of text and more creative instructors. In addition, our own literate lives can be elevated through the student partnerships we develop. But to participate in our communities of practice, we must surround ourselves with young adult books and be readers ourselves. Knowing the literature and being members of our communities of practice make us more knowledgeable about our own reading processes and what is behind the books (e.g., the scholarship and community that made the books possible). Our community is stronger if we are members of it, and to be good stewards, we must lead literate lives. As our communities of practice develop ideas, we can support their thinking by contributing this knowledge to the discussions and offering suggestions for places the entire community might look to strengthen their knowledge too.

Embracing this kind of immersion in YA literature and strengthening our individual and collective conceptions of our readerly selves allow us to better start, act, participate, and forward our *practice* alongside and with our communities—engaging locally and globally. We can use technology too to make our practices even more outward-facing. I intentionally conclude this book with this call for all of us to lead literate lives, and then I invite you to work with students to reflect on how your own communities of practice have the potential to use texts to strengthen your approach to teaching and to join in wider communities locally and globally. Thus, this chapter first looks inward to ourselves and then looks outward to opportunities for participatory practices in our class community of practice, our local communities, our global community, and with technology.

Teacher Stewards as Readers

As teacher stewards, we must be active readers who are able to contribute to the communities of practice we forge in our classrooms. The NCTE position statement (2018) reminds us that "teachers who are engaged readers do a better job of engaging students as readers" (xv). When we are reading regularly, just as we advocate for our students to do, we are reminded of the struggles and the triumphs that come with being a reader. When I struggle to identify characters, ponder the setting of a book, engage in a new or different mode or platform of reading (Garcia & O'Donnell-Allen, 2015), or wonder how I might revise a section of a book, I'm thinking like a reader. It's only by practicing and pushing myself as a reader in these ways that I can be a better steward of reading. Moreover, when I read an incredible book, I feel that undeniable burn to share it with others, to become a part of a community of readers that talks about these moments and shares texts that excite, push, or compel us. And I know I can be a member of that kind of community only if I'm engaging in the reading practices I genuinely believe make us people who seek to better ourselves and work toward a better world. I can't be the only member of the community of practice who isn't engaging in thinking deeply about reading, my readerly life, and the ways I might participate in my community.

One way you might join the community of readers in your classroom is by reading more openly during independent reading time and by regularly sharing during student sharing time the reading you do outside of school. This action reaffirms that reading practices aren't attached to school hours and that adults also continue these practices outside of the school building. Some teachers include a reading wall in their classrooms and use pictures or lists where students update what they're currently reading for other students across class periods. I recommend that you too update the wall with your own current texts. My rule of thumb is: If the students in my community of practice are doing something, I'm doing it too. Others in the school building might also offer contributions to the wall as guest posts, or the wall might be in a more public place in the school building or larger community. This wall could be a digital space as well, accessible by parents and school and community members.

Knowing the Books and What's Behind the Books

For teacher stewards to be strong YA readers, they need to know the literature: both the books and what's behind the books in the field of young adult literature. Knowing the literature itself requires us to read widely and regularly. With the explosion of YA literature, it can be hard to know where to start. In Figure 5.1, I offer suggestions of booklists, award lists, and review blogs for finding the most current good books. Students and teachers can access these lists to find texts of interest.

Scholarly Journals and Public Reviews of Texts

Scholarship also offers critical examinations of YA literature and its use in classrooms and libraries. You might read this scholarship regularly to stay current in the field *and* you can invite students to read the scholarship as well, as partners in learning in your community of practice. *The ALAN Review* is a peer-reviewed (refereed) scholarly journal devoted to a study of the literature. It's published three times per academic year and is read by teachers, librarians, university educators, authors, and publishers. (Note: If you attend the ALAN Workshop, a one-year membership of the journal is included in your registration.) The columns and articles support the learning and development of readers who are committed to this literature. The journal also often publishes the voices of YA authors. The research articles and resources of this journal have been invaluable to me as both a classroom teacher and a scholar, and they challenge me to be a better teacher and scholar. I make these journals available to students, and I share what I'm learning with our community of practice.

Figure 5.1. Booklists, award lists, and review blogs.

Booklists and Award Lists

American Indian Youth Literature Award (https://ailanet.org/activities/american-indian-youth-literature-award/)
Américas Award (http://claspprograms.org/americasaward)
Arab American Book Award (http://www.arabamericanmuseum.org/book-awards)
Asian/Pacific American Libraries Association Award (https://www.apalaweb.org/awards/literature-awards/)
Carter G. Woodson Book Awards (https://www.socialstudies.org/awards/woodson)
Children's Africana Book Awards (http://africaaccessreview.org/childrens-africana-book-awards/)
Cooperative Children's Book Center (CCBC) Multicultural Booklists (https://ccbc.education.wisc.edu/booklists/)
Coretta Scott King Book Awards (http://www.ala.org/emiert/cskbookawards)
Jane Addams Children's Book Award (http://www.janeaddamschildrensbookaward.org/)
Lambda Literary Award (http://www.lambdaliterary.org/awards)
Middle East Book Award (http://www.meoc.us/book-awards.html)
New Voices Award (https://www.leeandlow.com/writers-illustrators/new-voices-award)
Pura Belpré Award (http://www.ala.org/alsc/awardsgrants/bookmedia/belpremedal)
Rainbow Book List (https://glbtrt.ala.org/rainbowbooks/)
Schneider Family Book Award (http://www.ala.org/awardsgrants/schneider-family-book-award)
Social Justice Books (https://socialjusticebooks.org/)
Stonewall Book Awards (http://www.ala.org/awardsgrants/stonewall-book-awards-mike-morgan-larry-romans-children%E2%80%99s-young-adult-literature-award)
Sydney Taylor Book Award (https://jewishlibraries.org/Sydney_Taylor_Book_Award/)
Tomás Rivera Mexican American Children's Book Award (http://riverabookaward.org/)
We Need Diverse Books (http://weneeddiversebooks.org/)

Review Blogs

1000 Black Girl Books Resource Guide (http://grassrootscommunityfoundation.org/1000-black-girl-books-resource-guide/)
Africa Access (http://africaaccessreview.org/)
African American Literature Book Club (https://aalbc.com/)
American Indians in Children's Literature (https://americanindiansinchildrensliterature.blogspot.com/)
Association of Jewish Libraries (https://jewishlibraries.org/index.php)
The Brown Bookshelf (https://thebrownbookshelf.com/)
¡Colorín Colorado! (http://www.colorincolorado.org/books-authors/multicultural-literature)
Cynthia Leitich Smith's Teacher and Librarian Resources (http://cynthialeitichsmith.com/)
The Dark Fantastic (http://thedarkfantastic.blogspot.com/)
Disability in Kidlit (http://disabilityinkidlit.com/)
Edi Cotton Quilt (https://edicottonquilt.com/)
Fledgling (https://zettaelliott.wordpress.com/2011/11/20/2011-african-american-ya-mg-novels/)
Latinxs in Kid Lit (https://latinosinkidlit.com/)
LGBTQ Reads (https://lgbtqreads.com/)
Oyate (http://www.oyate.org/)
Reads Rainbow (https://readsrainbow.com/)
Rich in Color (www.richincolor.com)
Unleashing Readers (http://www.unleashingreaders.com/)

Other journals that feature YA literature include *Study and Scrutiny: Research on Young Adult Literature*, which is less pedagogical and focuses solely on research in YA literature (whereas *The ALAN Review* includes research, pedagogy, and resources). NCTE and the International Literacy Association (ILA) publish journals that focus on YA literature and its instruction; I frequently seek out articles in NCTE's *English Journal* and ILA's *Journal of Adolescent & Adult Literacy*.

Although it's important to consider how *we* can know more about the field, it's also important to encourage students to explore these scholarly journals and public reviews as well. Some years, based on interest, students have determined that exploring the critical literature would be a valuable part of their classroom experience and have worked it into their course design. As I detailed in the last chapter, students in my YA literature elective each choose a recent article from *The ALAN Review* and hold interactive presentations about the content to share with their peers. Through these journals and the award lists, booklists, and review blogs included in Figure 5.1, my students and I stay current with the newest literature and trends and are able to think deeply and complexly about the literature. These lists offer a place to continue our learning as we listen to others who are committed to this work.

Connecting with Authors, Colleagues, and Others in the Field

Young adult authors, teachers, librarians, publishers, and university educators have a strong presence across social media platforms. This allows teachers to stay connected with others doing similar work, and it helps us to intentionally connect our students as well. In my university YA literature course, we often examine the public posts written by the authors of the books we're reading so we can learn more about the authors. Many YA literature authors write during the day and post about second jobs or social activism, and these happenings appeal to students because they connect with the authors' writing. You might follow authors on social media to learn about their next books and publication news. Further, you might follow conference speakers who inspire you. For me, connecting with colleagues has been a snowball effect, and I have learned so much from others in the field.

The easy accessibility of authors is exciting as we come to understand that authors are people rather than mysteries behind the pages. More than once, my community of practice has tweeted or messaged an author on a social media platform, and almost every time the authors have responded. Many communities of practice have taken advantage of the accessibility of authors to book in-person or virtual events with them. In the following vignette, Jenny Cameron Paulsen describes how she applied for grant funding to get five authors to attend an all-school assembly she called Rock the Word. Although this wasn't attached to a community of practice, it was a schoolwide event that could be fostered in a community of practice that shares similar interests.

Inviting Authors to the Classroom

Jenny Cameron Paulsen
Cedar Falls Community School District, Cedar Falls, IA
Twitter and Instagram: @jennypaulsen555

The idea of a creative writing festival, which I had already been tossing around in my head, formed fully at the 2015 NCTE Annual Convention in Minneapolis. I attended a movie event where I met e. E. Charlton-Trujillo and Gia Gordon (previously published as C. G. Watson), the founders of Never Counted Out, an organization dedicated to empowering youth voice through the arts. This chance meeting, along with their support, led me to prepare a dream grant proposal: five authors meeting with all junior high students in Cedar Falls. I figured we should ask for the dream; we could always scale it back. Never Counted Out is available to help teachers with this kind of work at any time. Just visit http://nevercountedout.com/ and fill out the contact information.

Once I had a vision and help with grant writing, I needed a funding source. I asked many people in my community about local nonprofits with literacy goals. I personally contacted the people on my list, and I completed applications for those that seemed most promising. A local foundation generously granted full funding for the dream! This grant is limited to my area of the state of Iowa, but simple searching will create a list of strong leads for local (or even national) grant applications. Contact foundation staff personally to discuss how your goals align with their mission, and be sure to emphasize the connection of your project to the mission in the grant application.

Working with both junior high teacher librarians, we created a schedule with an all-school assembly followed by author sessions for each grade. EVERY student in grades 7 through 9 at both junior highs had the opportunity to learn from some of the best authors writing literature for young adults today, all passionate advocates for teen voice and empowerment.

Once we had our plan, we presented it to our administrators, who approved it immediately. We have strong support for literacy in our community, so we forged these connections, and we made sure not to interfere with lunch time. Students in our local university teaching program assisted at both junior high schools, while their English department sponsored an author signing event coordinated with our locally owned bookstore. Dream big, but seek local support and partnership. That's the secret to author visit success!

As a note, it's important to respect authors' private lives. We can tweet and reach out to authors publicly to praise their books when we, as a class, love what we read and want to share this with the world. But we should do so in a way that is careful not to invade an author's privacy. For instance, if I'm Facebook friends with an author, I should share only posts the author has shared publicly, not those they posted just to friends. This allows us to remain connected to those doing this work and also connect our students to learn more about and support their favorite authors.

Participatory Practices with Students to Build Literate Lives in Community

Thinking about our own reading processes, the YA books and the scholarship and community behind the books allow us to better support our community of practice. As a community, we can embark on a journey of revising and rewriting our conceptions of how to create classroom spaces that best support reading in collaborative and co-generated ways. This process is ongoing, and we regularly check in with our communities of practice to consider how we can better elevate our reading community and better engage with the world in participatory ways.

Over the last two decades, I have watched as my colleagues across schools and universities have engaged in classroom reading practices that deepen relationships to text, to each other, and to the world. I don't claim all of the practices in this section, and wherever possible, I cite who I believe to be the founder of an idea or practice. These approaches offer opportunities to increase our knowledge of books and also to engage in discussions about YA literature. As students focus on texts that push them toward authentic issues locally and globally, they discover a participatory environment in which to engage in critique of what they read and talk about texts in ways that move them toward productive community engagement.

Participatory Practices for Sharing Texts

While it is vital for us to flood our classrooms with high-quality, high-interest texts, the practices described in this section speak to the importance of allowing students to participate in the act of sharing new titles and talking about books. When we, as a community of practice, brainstorm the ways students can share and talk about texts, we have agreed to use some of the practices described below. Students should be empowered to build their own ideas for sharing texts too. One year, for instance, a student suggested that we design our own bookstore. We spent a class period designing a mural for the hallway to share titles with other students. Participatory practices like this offer opportunities to build community and learn more about the marketing and sale of YA literature; but we can't delve into the complexity of texts until we've built a strong community in which students feel that their interests and needs as readers are valued and that we've set our practices and goals. In this chapter, many of the activities allow us to talk about texts in our lives and look inward before we're able to consider looking outward locally, nationally, or globally—the *practice* of our community of practice.

Book Tastings

There are many popular classroom strategies connected to food and restaurants, such as book tastings, book bistros, or book cafés that can be used to build a community of readers who share new texts. Many of us eat communally with family and friends, and although schools vary in their willingness to permit food-related events on-site, book tastings and related reading experiences can be used with no real food at all. Each offers opportunities to bring students together to think about books and introduce themselves and each other to new titles.

During the first week of school, before we start talking about our needs and how we might be inspired to connect with community, I hold a book tasting as a starting activity. I group desks with different food items and ask students to talk about beloved books in relationship to food. Students sit in each of the groups of desks to think about how we think about texts. To do this activity, you might put grapes at one group of desks and ask students which foods are "healthy choices" and what they would consider to be a healthy reading choice. You might put cheese and crackers at another group of desks and ask students to share texts that are perceived as "fancy choices" and what they consider to be a fancy reading choice. Or you might use foods for binge choices. (This offers opportunities to discuss how we think about food too!) The book tasting was an activity I did as a university student in Wendy Glenn's course, and I still remember some of the rich discussions we had about the purpose and perceptions of text. If food isn't allowed in your school, you might use movies or some other category to achieve the same purpose.

Book Café

A book café can generate interest around new titles, topics, genres, award winners, book club choices, or other purposes. Groups of students sit with four or five titles, each representing a different meal course (appetizers, salads, entrees, desserts). They complete a menu during each course, and the students think about their purposes for the discussion (e.g., peritext, topic, interest). They co-generate the aspects they are looking for in their meal (tasting of each book), and they take notes on the menu. Just as they would in a restaurant, students "taste" each text. Students find the book café to be fun and engaging, and it feels like an elevated way to introduce new texts collaboratively rather than listening to one another give book talks.

Book Bistro

The book bistro (Kasten & Wilfong, 2005) is an activity I have suggested and used with both my high school and university communities of practice, and both groups loved the format as a way to talk about books and share titles in community. Once a month, I bring in tablecloths and centerpieces, students bring their own food (this isn't necessary if having food isn't permitted in your context), and everyone arrives at the book bistro with a book they want to share in a casual, relaxed environment. Kasten and Wilfong suggest asking students to complete a trifold brochure during the book bistro. The middle of the brochure features information they want to share about the books they brought, and they complete the left-hand and right-hand sides of the brochure as a sort of peer review of the books shared by individuals sitting to their direct left and right. Students are always thrilled about book bistro days; you might even turn on some soft music for a more bistro-like ambiance.

Book Talks

No matter the course—required or elective—I have never worked with a community of practice that hasn't incorporated book talks into the classroom structure. The members of your community of practice (including you) can do live book talks or prerecord yourselves on a platform like Flipgrid. Each student can select a day on the calendar to share the current book they are reading and love, or they can share a book they have previously read that they recommend to their classmates. You might also ask students to select a place or space in their community (another English class or somewhere locally) to do public book talks. Students enjoy returning to their middle schools or joining three to four other peers to share books with the community in a more public space, such as an outdoor mall. Although at first my students groan at the idea of participating in a public book talk, this is one of the aspects of the course that, years later, they continue to talk about as a powerful experience in which they publicly defined themselves as readers and reading advocates.

Book Pass

We can connect with our reading community by discovering new books together. You and your students might each sign out a big stack of new books from the library, or you could bring in a stack of books from a conference like the ALAN Workshop or the NCTE Annual Convention. Our community of practice sits in a circle, and we each grab a random book from the stack. We set a timer, and we each spend forty-five to sixty seconds with the book in front of us. We look at the peritext, read the summary, and read a page or two. When the timer goes off, we jot down titles of interest and rotate the books clockwise in the circle. Whenever your community is feeling a lull in their reading energy, you can do a book circle like this one, and in community you can learn new titles and add to your to-be-read lists.

Participatory Practices for Discussing Texts

Sharing texts ensures that each member of our community of practice always has a book in hand and a book on deck. This creates momentum and provides us with a weapon against the dreaded reading rut, those periods when we lose inspiration to read. Beyond sharing titles, you might also suggest to your community of practice how you could intentionally use participatory practices to discuss texts, building and strengthening your connected reading community. As Muhammad (2020) suggests, learners have a responsibility not only to themselves but also to each other. Good books push our communities of practice forward, encourage meaningful conversations, and prompt brainstorming about how we enact social change. I find students enjoy mixing up the ways they talk about books, and these supportive structures ignite conversations that get them started on this thinking and brainstorming. Some of the instructional practices your community of practice might use to encourage book discussions follow.

Student-Led Discussion Circles and Fishbowls

Before any discussion, I ask students to contribute ideas or questions to guide the conversation. They can write these ideas on slips of paper or jot them down in their notebooks. Then, whenever the conversation needs renewed energy, students can contribute new ideas for discussion. Fishbowls operate similarly. You might ask four or five students to sit in an inner circle while the other students sit in an outer circle. The inner circle discusses a topic from the student-generated ideas and questions. When a student from the outer circle wants to contribute to the conversation, they tap a shoulder and replace a student in the inner circle who has made at least two comments. Students in the outer circle can take notes of conversation highlights.

Socratic Seminars

The Socratic seminar is grounded in Socrates's valuing of inquiry over knowledge. Students sit in an inner or an outer circle. The inner circle closely examines and asks questions of the text. These might include big picture questions, such as those related to text and author context, or close reading questions, such as the purpose of specific lines in the text. Each inner circle student is paired with an outer circle student who acts as their coach. At several points, take a break so the pair can talk about how the inner circle student is doing. The outer circle student can offer ideas and support. Socratic seminars allow students to think deeply about texts and the questions they ask as they read texts. This approach also helps students listen carefully to each other and value their peers' contributions. You may need to begin as the facilitator if students aren't accustomed to this instructional approach, but the aim is for students to guide and lead the discussion. Assessment of Socratic seminars often includes reflective writing of the experience, domain, and text(s).

Jigsawing Books

You might be familiar with the jigsaw instructional approach, which is commonly used to discuss multiple articles. Students in my community of practice have also used this approach to discuss independent or shared texts, as well. If you're unfamiliar with the method: Students spend time in their "expert" group of students who read the same article to discuss a central class question or domain and to determine shared learnings gleaned from their article. Students in these groups are then each assigned a letter. If you have six students in group 1, while they are conversing, assign them letters A, B, C, D, E, and F on the board. In group 2, assign students letters A, B, C, D, E, and F again. This continues for all of the groups. The students then move from their "expert" groups into "mixed expert" groups, so "A" students, "B" students, etc., meet. Each student in the new group has read a different text and can contribute to the conversation about the domain. If any group has more students than other groups, students can double up—in other words, two students may be from the same original home group. The idea is that students have a home group and then they share this knowledge across groups, typically discussing a central domain across texts.

Another way we've used jigsawing as an instructional strategy is to co-generate several topics for discussion about a shared text. These might include specific passages of interest, ideas for discussion (e.g., themes, characters, central topics within the text), or local or global applications of and potential for the text. Students meet in their "expert" groups. Then, in the "mixed expert" groups, students take ownership of their topic or theme and lead a small discussion about the topics. Jigsawing can be used with independent novels as well. For instance, "expert" groups might each select a different short narrative text to connect to the novels, or they might each select a discussion topic about writer's craft. Then, in "mixed expert" groups, students make larger connections to their own novels. The jigsawing strategy moves away from a teacher-directed approach, opening up conversations for students to generate domains of interest to them and their communities.

Concentric Circles (or Inside/Outside Circle)

As with the previous instructional approaches, your community of practice might begin concentric circles with students submitting questions or domains of interest on slips of paper. Divide the class in half, with half of the students in an inside circle and half in an outside circle. The two circles face each other, pairing one inside and one outside student, and students speak for two to three minutes about a topic (What was your favorite part from the reading? What is your book about? What aspect of the author's craft is most compelling to you?). Following this discussion, one of the circles rotates clockwise or counterclockwise, and a member of your community of practice can offer a new topic. My more introverted students value this instructional approach because they are able to talk independently with one peer at a time rather than with the entire class. We can talk about a breadth of several different domains in a short period of time, helping us gauge student interest in some of these domains. If there's an odd number of students, we either group two students together, or I step outside of the circle.

Give One, Get One

For this discussion strategy, students begin by folding their papers in half lengthwise (hot dog style). In the left-hand column, they write down everything they learned from a reading, everything they found interesting or compelling, or quotes that inspired them. Whatever the focus, they should be able to generate a lot of ideas in that column. Then they write the numbers 1 through 10 in the right-hand column. Their job is to chat with ten peers in the community of practice and to fill in ten ideas (one from each peer) that they didn't write in their own left-hand column. This activity inspires great conversation and allows students to think deeply about their own learnings and perspectives as well as those of their peers. I find that this activity, more than any other, generates a lot of laughter and enjoyment.

Sticky Note Walk

For this instructional approach, students can co-create four to six major discussion questions or ideas related to a domain of interest about the shared reading or about independent reading texts. These questions can be posted on papers plastered on the classroom walls. In groups, students walk to one of the questions and discuss the topic. After some time for thinking, one of the group members writes one highlight of their conversation on a sticky note (each group with a different color) and attach it to the wall or paper with the discussion question on it. The groups rotate around the room to read previous comments and discuss each question, adding something new each time. When a group reaches the final question, following this last discussion one person shares out one sticky note from a previous group attached to the discussion question. This lets us discuss topics (or domains) with smaller groups while still reading and learning about others' perspectives.

Pass the Ideas

For this strategy, we split into small groups, each working with a large sheet of paper. We work together to assign each group a different character, topic, or domain of interest, and we develop a central question for all groups to consider. For instance, each group might pick a character from a shared novel, and then we think together to design a question that allows us to contemplate a different domain (e.g., What do we know about the domains thus far, and what do we want to learn?). In their groups, students write notes, draw, list ideas, or create in any medium of interest. Next, we pass the big sheets of paper with the ideas clockwise to the next group. They read the ideas of the previous group and add their own. Then we ask a new question that allows us to explore more deeply the domains (e.g., What areas of support could we explore to learn more?). Students write notes again, and you can keep passing the big sheets of paper with ideas across groups. By the end, we have built a whole-class, complex understanding of several different potential domains for exploration. We often post these on my classroom walls. I find that this activity takes practice, but with time, students feel more confident contributing questions as thinking points, which makes the process more engaging and student-centered.

Four Corners

Students are often accustomed to anticipation guides that ask them to strongly agree, agree, disagree, or strongly disagree with topics or ideas in a text. With four corners, place a sign in each corner of the room for each level of agreement and ask students to walk to the corner of the room that reflects their opinion. (Alternatively, if you don't like using four corners, you can ask students to stand along a line of a spectrum from strongly agree to strongly disagree that reflects their agreement with an idea). As students speak about their opinions, I encourage them to move if their opinion shifts during the conversation. In a community of practice, this approach isn't limited to books; the community might use it to discuss their perceptions of reading and literacy, for instance. A student might say, "An educated reader has read many canonical texts." Thinking about reading—our own processes and practices and commonly held assumptions—offers students an ownership over the concept of reading and encourages their voices in a discussion. These discussion topics can be centered on a domain to build understandings within the community.

Write Five

Whenever there is space for a large conversation, I suggest to the community of practice that we use "write five." After reading a whole-class text, for instance, we might all write five ______. This blank might include five impressions of the text, five lines that inspired them, five related domains we could study, or five connections to the community. Then students find a peer and discuss the ten ideas across their two papers, reducing the collaborative list to five of their best ideas (these ten can be synthesized across their lists and rewritten as a new five). Two pairs of students then join each other to make a group of four. They synthesize their ideas down to a collective five again. At this point, I typically have students report out (most often writing their lists on the board), and we synthesize the lists into a final five as a class (often with a heated debate). This strategy is useful because it allows students to synthesize ideas and determine the most essential, important concepts while also considering peers' perspectives.

Some days our community of practice chats freely, but these semi-structured discussion strategies allow us to creatively chat about books more deeply and meaningfully. They make discussions more exciting and help our class bond and build community. Many of the strategies involve movement to energize us. Trying out new ways of talking about texts, domains, and connections to community builds a foundation and rapport as we look inward before we look outward together.

Participatory Practices with Students to Leverage Community Locally

A next step after building community in your classroom is toward engaging with community locally. Students might, for instance, identify community needs and leverage YA literature to act on these needs by going out into the community. Local communities are rich with opportunities for engagement, and your classroom community of practice might even engage with existing initiatives, such as a local LGBTQ+ youth organization or an effort to combat food insecurity in your community. Other scholars suggest how we might leverage community by inviting people into the classroom—either in person or virtually. Once we define our domain(s) together, our community of practice determines not only the texts we will study but also the experts we will seek to invite.

One domain that has emerged frequently in my communities of practice is a desire to support literacy through relationships and partnerships with their local community. Some ways that I've included my own community as a high school teacher (and a few more recently as a university professor) have included:

- Linking my high school students with younger students to read and share books and titles;
- Hosting pop-up, live book talks and reading circles around town in public spaces;
- Responding to current events with community-wide readings, discussions, and action plans for change;
- Helping students create and paint a mural in their community;
- Facilitating a student-led book fair for which students networked and built connections with community partners;
- Hosting a half-day local radio session related to literacy and human rights;
- Hosting a public ice cream social to share new book titles and fund future classroom titles; and
- Inviting guests (e.g., administration, Board of Education members, community members) to read shared YA texts and join conversations relevant to the community for specific topics of interest.

It's important to remember that you don't need to (and shouldn't) make these decisions alone. Students work within their community of practice to identify community needs and their interests. Then you can work collaboratively to identify ways your classroom can include and work with the community in participatory ways as forms of practice.

Participatory Practices with Students to Leverage Community Globally

Young adult literature offers opportunities to think about the global systems and processes that are critical for our world. Students can work to understand how they are situated historically and interculturally within global and comparative contexts and perspectives. Young adult literature offers a communication tool for students to talk, think, and act within and across differences; engage in conversations about global issues; and seek out opportunities to change the world.

One way you can intentionally select texts that offer these opportunities for critical engagement and dialogue about global issues is by asking students to engage with the Global Goals for Sustainable Development (https://globalgoals.org); the organization Project Everyone offers lesson ideas for these goals (https://worldslargestlesson.globalgoals.org). Figure 5.2 shares a black-and-white image

Figure 5.2. The global goals for sustainable development. (Used with permission from Project Everyone.)

of the Global Goals, but I recommend printing the colored images offered on the website.

My communities of practice have used these goals in two ways. The first is to identify YA literature students are interested in reading and then connect topics from the texts with global goals. The second is to start with the global goals and then match YA texts with those goals. Regardless, we also always brainstorm global goals not pictured in the graphic. For me, selecting from a list isn't as powerful as *choosing* a goal of interest. When there has been interest in working with the global goals, I, as steward, have printed out the goals and taped them to the walls around the room. The students grab a notebook, walk to a goal of interest, and sit with it for a while. If another person walks to the same goal, they might engage in a conversation about the goal. Some questions they might ponder as they sit with the goals (and these questions were co-generated with a college community of practice I worked with):

- What might I study if I wanted to learn more about this goal?
- Who might help me learn more about this global goal?

- What young adult texts might offer me new understandings of this goal?
- How might I participate locally and globally to work toward change?

If the community of practice is interested, we incorporate the Global Goals for Sustainable Development into our classroom. As teacher steward, it has been fascinating to watch the very different ways the students use this graphic to determine their involvement and form of *practice*. It's been equally fascinating to examine how certain goals trend and which goals interest students. For instance, recently, amid the COVID-19 pandemic, Good Health and Well-Being, a goal that was *never* selected by previous students, has become more prominent. When I moved from Connecticut to Colorado, I noticed students were more interested in the goals related to environmental, water, and sustainability concerns. No matter the goal, students never seem to struggle to find one that interests them. We have had rich discussions about which goals seem more central in their worldviews and why this might be.

Independently or in groups, students select a global goal (which becomes their domain of study) and read YA texts related to that goal. They identify key stakeholders to interview and use their YA texts to understand the domain more deeply. The summative assessment has differed over the years. One year my students created campaigns using technology; another year we focused on writing letters to representatives. Whatever the end product (the practice), our aim is to interact and engage globally in meaningful ways and to use our knowledge to develop forms of practice that play an active role both locally and globally to enact change.

Participatory Practices with Students to Leverage Community with Technology

As we think about our global connections, it's impossible not to consider how we can and do use technology in our classrooms. Technology offers opportunities for us to be more active participants in our community both locally and globally as we examine YA literature and deepen connections with others.

Connecting with Technology and Using Technology in the Classroom

Students can connect nationally and internationally with other readers and thinkers of YA literature. Navigating the changing world means that we are preparing our students for careers that will likely include some level of technological integration. Technology offers options that elevate classroom instruction and a lens to engage with YA literature.

One way that your students might look outward at the world of books is to read and analyze public reviews of texts and analyze why certain texts are marketed more than others and how this might affect their community. Look at *Booklist*, *The Bulletin of the Center for Children's Books*, the *Horn Book*, *Kirkus Reviews*, *Publishers Weekly*, *School Library Journal*, and *VOYA* (Voice of Youth Advocates) to consider purposes and processes for sharing starred reviews of young adult texts. In these publications, book reviews provide a descriptive summary (often written by a single reviewer), and a book that is considered noteworthy receives a starred review. The students and I discuss the potential complications and implications of this practice. For instance, starred reviews are subjective and often come down to the taste of a reader (Bluemle, 2011). Evaluating the starred review process and engaging with these publications online lets students be critics who look at how systems and processes operate in the literary world. Book reviews impact how books are ordered (by acquisitions teams at libraries with consideration of books' stars) and how they appear on search lists for websites. They affect which books face outward at some bookstores. They also impact which books even make it into the community through libraries and bookstores. You might look at titles from previous years and discuss how book reviews impact sales and what we, the consumers, read. I ask students to examine published book reviews and to consider how these reviews might impact a book's reception, both negatively and positively, and how this might be problematic. These discussions, which include analyses of book trends and consideration of why we read what we read and how the world filters the books that reach us, improve our skills as critical consumers of literature and members of the field.

One way for students to use technology as critical readers is through a Mock Book Award program, where they share their thinking virtually and build community as readers with valuable input. When students engage in a Mock Book Award, they read books (as a book award committee would) to evaluate and determine a winner for a well-known award. I've seen Mock Award programs adapted to elementary, middle, and high school, and all were successful in increasing students' interest in reading and generating excitement about new releases and the literary world in general. In the following vignette, Beth Shaum shares how a Mock Caldecott Award program increases students' emotional investment in reading and in the readerly world. I've seen middle and high school teachers design Mock Caldecott and Mock Newbery programs with picture books, and students had powerful discussions about book structure, peritext, authors' craft, illustrator's craft, and literary merit. In the subsequent vignette, Emma Carbone describes her process for designing a Mock Printz for her librarians as professional development and how this process can be applied to classrooms. With Emma's program, a central team (which could be a class, a book club, or a group of volunteers) evaluates new releases and selects a shortlist for everyone to read. The process of selecting books requires the team to research sources on the internet to learn about the newest titles that are favored to win the awards. This program could be adapted to include community members, teachers in the building, and administrators to generate a school- and community-wide Mock Book Award. You might publish your Mock Book Award results on social media to generate excitement before the official book award announcements (in January for the ALA Youth Media Awards). I know several teachers who have done Mock Book Awards as after-school programs, and they've hosted an in-school field trip on the day of the award announcements.

Mock Book Awards and Student Emotional Investment

Beth Shaum
St. Francis of Assisi Catholic School, Ann Arbor, Michigan
Instagram: teacherlibrarianbeth

Doing mock awards with students is a great way to get them excited and reading books they never would have picked up otherwise. Not only are the books that you include in your mock reading lists a way to stretch their reading muscles, but once the awards are announced, students are sure to scramble to read any of the books that were not included in your list.

As a K–8 librarian, every year I host a Mock Caldecott Award for the entire school. Over the course of a couple months, I read students a series of twelve to fifteen picture books that were published during that year, and then in January students vote for the book they think will win. Then, in the week that the ALA Youth Media Awards are announced, I show students in all of the classes the recorded webcast so they can see the variety of awards that are given out.

Every year I inevitably have students who see books that are announced as award winners and ask me, "Do we have that book in the library? No? Can we get it?" Which always reminds me why I do mock awards in the first place. Students learn about the history of these awards, delve into the process of what being on an award jury is like, and, most important, get emotionally invested in these books. Whether their favorite wins or doesn't, their emotional reactions, whether elation or disappointment, are visible and heartfelt.

Organizing a Mock Printz at Your Library

Emma Carbone
Brooklyn Public Library, Brooklyn, NY
http://missprint.wordpress.com
Twitter: miss_print
Instagram: missprint_

My library system hosts a yearly Mock Printz book discussion as a professional development opportunity to help staff build their readers' advisory frameworks and to introduce them to recently published titles. This is a program that can be easily adapted at the classroom level for teachers seeking to host a Mock Printz themselves. Alternately, the school library could serve as a partner in the process. In my program, library staff discuss a preselected shortlist and vote for a winner and two honor titles; students could select this list of titles together.

Timeline

In my system, the Mock Printz is organized by the YA Book Showcase Committee, which consists of approximately twelve YA librarians. The committee's responsibilities include reading and evaluating newly released books for potential inclusion in the Mock Printz program, as well as presenting at and participating in committee-run programs, including new book presentations and book discussions. A Teen Advisory Board, Young Adult Literature course, English language arts class, or book club could also handle Mock Printz prep and book shortlist selection.

Printz results are announced at the ALA Midwinter Conference, which is usually held in January. Your Mock Printz should end one to two weeks before the conference in order to have your Mock Printz results before the actual Printz winner and honor lists are announced. Plan to announce your shortlist in November to give participants and presenters plenty of time to read and prepare.

Choose Your Longlist

To help focus choices for your shortlist, start with a running list of recommendations, books by previous winners and honorees, and titles receiving a lot of attention. Here are some ways you can start building out your Mock Printz Longlist:

1. **Ask for Suggestions:** As the committee chair, I ask the YA Book Showcase members around September to share any books they've read that seem Printz-worthy based on the official Printz criteria (www.ala.org/yalsa/booklistsawards/bookawards/printzaward/aboutprintz/criteria), which we compile in a spreadsheet.

2. **Look for Stars:** Since the official Printz criteria emphasize demonstrated literary merit, keep an eye on starred reviews from professional journals. You can find this information at online book retailer sites like Barnes & Noble's as well as through library databases, including NoveList, and directly from review journals such as *School Library Journal, Publisher's Weekly,* and *Kirkus.*

3. **"Best of" Lists:** *Kirkus, Publisher's Weekly, School Library Journal,* and numerous other publications release yearly best book lists. The finalists for the National Book Award (www.nationalbook.org/), Kirkus Prize (www.kirkusreviews.com/prize/), and YALSA's Morris Award (www.ala.org/yalsa/morris-award) and Nonfiction Award (www.ala.org/yalsa/nonfiction-award) are also helpful if they are announced early enough.

Finalize Your Shortlist

Depending on the length of your discussion and the length of the books, your shortlist should be between four and six books. If you plan to select your shortlist with a smaller group discussion, budget at least two hours for the process.

Your shortlist should feature a mix of genres and formats, including contemporary fiction, sci-fi/fantasy, nonfiction, graphic novel, historical fiction, etc. You may also want to look for debuts and books from smaller publishers. The actual Printz isn't always this well rounded, but variety better ensures that something will appeal to everyone and introduces participants to examples of genres they may not normally read.

Your final shortlist should be an inclusive, balanced list of authors and protagonists in terms of aspects such as gender identity, sexuality, cultural background, and life experiences as varied as your vibrant library community and beyond. Try to make sure some of your titles are available as e-books and/or audiobooks so that the shortlist is as accessible as possible to participants.

I start every shortlist discussion by asking committee members if anything should immediately be removed, including books that won't be available at the library before the Mock Printz. If a majority agrees, the title is removed. After that quick elimination round, committee members vote for their top five choices. Any book that has one or no votes is eliminated in each round. This process continues until the shortlist can be determined. Once the shortlist is announced, committee members volunteer to present each title.

Organize Your Mock Printz Program

Start your Mock Printz by explaining the official Printz criteria and the evening's agenda. At my Mock Printz, committee members then share five-minute presentations on how each book fulfills those criteria and relevant details such as starred reviews or award nominations. After each five-minute presentation, allot ten minutes of discussion with an additional ten minutes for final thoughts before voting.

Voting is modeled on the actual Printz's weighted voting, with first, second, and third place choices on the ballot. First place gets three points, second place gets two points, third place gets one point. If a title receives five votes for first place, that would be multiplied by three for a total of fifteen points, and so on. The book with the highest total score is the winner, with the next lowest being an honor title. The actual Printz would also need a specific majority of votes to be declared the winner, but time limitations may prevent run-off votes at your Mock Printz.

And the Winner Is . . .

After votes are tallied, announce your Mock Printz winner and honor titles at your program event or in your class. You can share the results with the rest of your library or community via display or social media too. Then wait to see how your choices compare to the actual Printz results.

Students should have access to the most recent technology related to reading. New educational technology emerges regularly, and as a teacher steward, I try to position this as an exciting rather than an overwhelming reality. You can invite *students* to identify, explore, and use technology that fits their needs and interests centered on a domain. For instance, one of my communities of practice used technology as a main component of their independent reading *practice*. One student opted to use Minecraft to do world building related to his text's setting. Another student built a video game that reflected the mood of and conflict in his text. A third student used a virtual reality program to build a classroom. Others used apps and websites that were unfamiliar to me. We spent many days workshopping and exploring apps and technology together to help students find platforms and tools that were good fits for their needs. More than once, a student needed help learning a platform, website, or app that was unfamiliar to me. With plenty of workshop time and a lot of peer support, we navigated these new technologies, significantly increasing our muscles and skills as we learned so much about available technologies for extending our thinking and sharing our work. In the final vignette, teacher L. E. Oldham shares opportunities for trusting students to become creators of content who use technology in critical ways.

Critical Use of Technology in Teaching YA Literature

L. E. Oldham
Deming Public Schools, Deming, NM
Instagram and Twitter: @thebooksupplier

When I started teaching YA literature and integrating technology into my reader responses, it looked like a series of slides with mock social networking site templates. Although this activity asked students to engage with character, plot, and how these two story elements interacted with each other, it didn't require students to engage with technology in a meaningful or authentic way.

Engaging critically with technology in the teaching of YA literature, especially if through a reader-response approach, requires more than adding information to a prefabricated template. It requires students to interrogate how they construct meaning from the texts they read and determine how best to use technology to create a new text that demonstrates their interaction with the source text.

There are a myriad of apps, websites, and programs, both existing and those that are yet to be conceived of, that allow for what I was missing: space for students to interact with one another and with YA literature in critical, meaningful ways.

The authentic ways might include:

- using video message boards to create original content or analyze literature;
- designing zines about texts or about pertinent themes in a text that connect the contexts of the novels to current sociopolitical issues;
- writing, producing, and publishing podcasts (e.g., narrative, informational, literary criticism) with specific consideration not only for content, but also for sound design and what their choice of sound effects and music, or lack thereof, communicates to their audience; or
- using technology to connect with other students across the world, and organizing action against the injustices they learn about as they make connections between the YA literature they read and the current world.

These are only a few examples. At its heart, integrating technology critically with the teaching of young adult literature is about designing opportunities for students to become not only creators of content but also creators of content who consider their purpose and audience, and then select the best methods and tools to create that content for that audience.

> In these examples, more of the onus is on the students to create, to inform, and to build meaning with others about the connections they're making in the texts they read. And because these experiences have the potential to be more meaningful and authentic, they're also motivating in that, depending on the prompt, they can help students see how reading literature is not only reading the word but also reading the world (Freire & Macedo, 1987).

As L. E. Oldham describes, technology isn't about finding the newest, fanciest app—rather, technology should be used in intentional ways to elevate the classroom experience and forward the *practice*, build connections, and trust in young people to think critically about texts. Technology can elevate a classroom experience to build connections to content. Deepening our thinking about literature and situating ourselves and our students in the field should be tied to intentional inclusion of technology as a tool for learning and sharing. You need not be an expert in all available technologies to integrate technology into your classroom, because you are just one member of the community of practice. I have found that students are often willing partners and leaders in learning about technologies, and this exploration process benefits us all as we think critically about audience, purpose, and form.

Conclusion

As we teach young adult literature, we can consider our own reading processes and what we know about the literature and the field. This knowledge and the students' knowledge help foster the community of practice in our classrooms, as well as our engagement locally and globally. YA literature is powerful in the connections it allows us to make. We ask questions of ourselves and to enrich our understandings of who we are, and we also consider how we are readers, learners, and thinkers situated in context. As L. E. Oldham notes, this literature gives us permission and encourages us to read the word and also the world (Freire & Macedo, 1987) by engaging with this context in meaningful ways. It offers potential in its power to help us understand and think about others and the local and global issues that matter to us and our communities. The relevance of this literature makes classrooms authentic spaces that call for engaged pedagogical approaches. As we reimagine our classroom spaces—rattling the cage and using the many hands around us—we are able to consider our place in the world and also transform ourselves every time we open a young adult text. And the experience is quite magnificent.

Annotated Bibliography

This is a nonexhaustive list of books that I have found helpful in my journey to challenge traditional classroom spaces with young adult literature. I refer to these texts regularly to extend and deepen my thinking.

Teacher Books to Extend Thinking and Inspire

Baker-Bell, April
Linguistic Justice: Black Language, Literacy, Identity, and Pedagogy
Routledge and National Council of Teachers of English, 2020

Baker-Bell works to dismantle Anti-Black Linguistic Racism through a pedagogical approach that centers the linguistic, cultural, racial, intellectual, and self-confidence needs of Black students. Using ethnographic examples and bridging research, theory, and practice, this text explores how traditional instruction commits linguistic oppression and then outlines pedagogical approaches for implementing liberatory instructional practices.

Blackburn, Molly V., Caroline T. Clark, and Wayne J. Martino, editors
Queer and Trans Perspectives on Teaching LGBT-Themed Texts in Schools
Routledge, 2018

This edited collection deepens understandings about teaching LGBT-themed texts in classrooms. Chapters move beyond LGBT-inclusivity to focus on how we can queer texts with LGBT themes to better inform our literacy instruction. The chapters work together to offer a rich understanding of how we might deepen our thinking and offer more complex conversations and conceptualizations of LGBT-themed texts in our classrooms.

Boerman-Cornell, William, and Jung Kim
Using Graphic Novels in the English Language Arts Classroom
Bloomsbury, 2020

This text shares how we read, study, and interpret graphic novels and also how we can use research about graphic novels to share effective methods for instruction. Using several popular, successful, and strong examples of graphic novels, the text offers planning and instructional suggestions and recommendations for teachers.

Borsheim-Black, Carlin, and Sophia Tatiana Sarigianides
Letting Go of Literary Whiteness: Antiracist Literature Instruction for White Students
Teachers College Press, 2019

Each chapter of this text offers a different aspect of antiracist literature instruction in schools. It focuses on racial literacy and includes examples of literature, suggestions for text selection, strategies for literacy instruction, analyses of Whiteness in the canon, and opportunities for assessment design. The authors break down complex ideas about antiracist literature instruction to engage readers in critical thinking and design, including practical suggestions for teacher-readers.

Buehler, Jennifer
Teaching Reading with YA Literature: Complex Texts, Complex Lives
National Council of Teachers of English, 2016

Teaching Reading with YA Literature uses vignettes and lessons to help teachers consider their own approaches to teaching YA literature as a way to encourage all students to be enthusiastic readers. The book shares strategies for building a classroom reading community, matching students with texts, and teaching in ways that foster complexity, agency, and autonomy. Buehler's book complements this text in its focus on the complexity of YA literature.

Dail, Jennifer S., Shelbie Witte, and Steven T. Bickmore, editors
Toward a More Visual Literacy: Shifting the Paradigm with Digital Tools and Young Adult Literature
Rowman & Littlefield, 2018

With a strong argument for including technology and multimodal texts in the literacies we teach in our schools, this text provides suggestions for expanding and implementing multiple modes of literacy in the classroom. It offers digital tools for engaging in critical conversations and considerations of how students make meaning from text, visualize digitally, engage socially, and inquire critically and deeply.

Gallagher, Kelly
Deeper Reading: Comprehending Challenging Texts, 4–12
Stenhouse, 2004

Focusing on grades 4–12, this text offers strategies for deepening comprehension of and reflection on challenging texts using the concept of reading in drafts, a practice that encourages students to reread to create more meaning. The literacy-based understandings provided in this book can be used in course design to work with students on creating deeper understandings of the texts we read.

Garcia, Antero, and Cindy O'Donnell-Allen
Pose, Wobble, Flow: A Culturally Proactive Approach to Literacy Instruction
Teachers College Press, 2015
As we grow as educators and challenge our thinking, we can commit ourselves to six culturally proactive teaching "poses" to meet the needs of students, "wobble" and adapt our instruction, and "flow" in flexible, positive ways to address these challenges. This book offers strategies and resources for the common wobbles we encounter as teachers to allow us to adapt our pedagogy each year.

Ginsberg, Ricki, and Wendy J. Glenn, editors
Engaging with Multicultural YA Literature in the Secondary Classroom: Critical Approaches for Critical Educators
Routledge, 2019

Each chapter of this coedited text offers a critical approach for teaching YA literature and the classroom strategies to do so. Individual chapters focus on a different central text as an exemplar and provide specific pedagogical activities that can be applied to other books. The text bridges theory and practice to allow teachers to explore key topics such as culture, (dis)ability, ethnicity, gender, immigration, race, sexual orientation, and social class.

Greathouse, Paula, and Victor Malo-Juvera, editors
Young Adult and Canonical Literature: Pairing and Teaching, Vols. I and II
Rowman & Littlefield, 2021

Greathouse and Malo-Juvera's two edited volumes offer concrete, practical pedagogical ideas for pairing young adult texts with canonical literature to explore themes and topics in ways that avoid centering the canonical texts. These chapters start with an idea or topic rather than a specific text, and the ideas can be used or adapted to think about how we bridge texts thoughtfully and with intention.

Kinloch, Valerie, Tanja Burkhard, and Carlotta Penn, editors
Race, Justice, and Activism in Literacy Instruction
Teachers College Press, 2019

This edited collection focuses on critical literacy as it intersects with race, justice, and activism in the classroom to promote social change. It combines theory and practice, and chapters provide different inspiring examples of engagement and student activism in schools and communities.

Love, Bettina L.
We Want to Do More Than Survive: Abolitionist Teaching and the Pursuit of Educational Freedom
Beacon Press, 2019

This text integrates story, research, and history to conceptualize how the methods of abolitionists can be used to promote sustainable change in schools and educational justice. Readers will consider how they might civically engage their students and enact justice within and outside of their classrooms.

Miller, Donalyn, with Susan Kelley
Reading in the Wild: The Book Whisperer's Keys to Cultivating Lifelong Reading Habits
Jossey-Bass, 2013

This book highlights survey responses from students and adult readers and extends the conversation of Miller's other popular book, *The Book Whisperer*, by sharing five key reading habits that can help students develop a lifelong love of reading. Each of the reading habits explored is based in a conception of what "wild readers" do and includes strategies, lesson plans, and assessment.

Minor, Cornelius
We Got This: Equity, Access, and the Quest to Be Who Our Students Need Us to Be
Heinemann, 2019

Minor focuses on how listening to kids and doing so authentically allows us to move toward more equitable instruction. The text includes specific strategies for planning and revising lessons for access and equity, grouping students, building community, making curriculum work for kids, and advocating for classroom and schoolwide changes.

Mirra, Nicole
Educating for Empathy: Literacy Learning and Civic Engagement
Teachers College Press and National Writing Project, 2018

This text proposes a model for critical civic empathy as a framework for thinking about the purposes of literacy education and for developing empathy and civic engagement in our classrooms. It offers authentic examples from various schools that synthesize theory and practice.

Muhammad, Gholdy
Cultivating Genius: An Equity Framework for Culturally and Historically Responsive Literacy
Scholastic, 2020

Using an equity framework, Muhammad offers suggestions for culturally and historically responsive literacy practices that build on theory and develop students' identities, skills, intellect, and criticality. The text uses historical understandings to promote excellence in literacy instruction.

Paris, Django, and H. Samy Alim, editors
Culturally Sustaining Pedagogies: Teaching and Learning for Justice in a Changing World
Teachers College Press, 2017

This book conceptualizes how teachers can implement culturally sustaining pedagogies in order to change classrooms, schools, and the world. The first chapter offers a loving critique and extension of culturally relevant pedagogies and provides a framework for sustaining communities of color. Subsequent chapters provide examples of this work in various school contexts that serve as inspiration for teachers seeking educational justice.

Richmond, Kia Jane
Mental Illness in Young Adult Literature: Exploring Real Struggles through Fictional Characters
Libraries Unlimited, 2018

In its examination of portrayals of mental illness in YA literature, this book offers suggestions for teachers, librarians, and mental health professionals who want to support young people. Each chapter offers a description of and demographic information on a mental illness, its depictions in young adult literature, strategies for teachers, and available resources.

Sabzalian, Leilani
Indigenous Children's Survivance in Public Schools
Routledge, 2019

This text pushes against the colonialism that still exists in schools and shares survivance stories that offer complex understandings of educational issues for Native students in classrooms. Teachers will develop anticolonial literacies to support Native students and learn how to counter deficit perspectives and colonial systems and practices.

Serravallo, Jennifer
The Reading Strategies Book: Your Everything Guide to Developing Skilled Readers
Heinemann, 2015

Serravallo's K–8 resource book offers a host of practical, step-by-step instructions with tips and examples for reading strategies that can be adapted by teachers to meet the needs of their own students. The three hundred strategies in this book are literacy-based and can be mapped onto a variety of course designs, rigid or flexible, to improve students' reading skills.

Thomas, Ebony Elizabeth
The Dark Fantastic: Race and the Imagination from Harry Potter to the Hunger Games
New York University Press, 2020

In her exploration of race in YA speculative fiction, Thomas shares how stories can offer escape to both real and imagined worlds. This book not only discusses in depth the diversity crisis in young adult literature, but it also (re)frames readers' understandings to reveal the great possibilities and intersections of race and speculative fiction within and beyond the classroom.

Westman, Lisa
Student-Driven Differentiation: 8 Steps to Harmonize Learning in the Classroom
Corwin, 2018

Broken down into eight steps, this book offers discussion and suggestions about how teachers can better differentiate their instruction to add more voice and choice in content, process, product, and environment. Teachers can apply the strategies in this book to plan and implement any lesson or assessment in any context.

YA Texts to Extend Thinking and Inspire

As noted in Chapter 5, to teach young adult literature, we must read often and always. In Figure 5.2 on page 129, I share award lists and booklists that review and identify some of the exceptional recent YA titles. I recommend checking these lists regularly and following the suggestions offered in Chapter 5 to identify and read new titles in the field.

Websites to Extend Thinking and Inspire

Assembly on Literature for Adolescents of NCTE (ALAN)

www.alan-ya.org
This assembly focuses on promoting communication and cooperation among teachers, librarians, university educators, publishers, authors, and others who have a shared interest in promoting YA literature. ALAN hosts social media pages and groups that are free to join. Members can read the newest scholarly issue of *The ALAN Review*, apply for grants to fund projects, read publications and the latest information about YA literature, as well as connect and network with others who have a special interest in this literature.

National Council of Teachers of English (NCTE)

www.ncte.org
This professional organization for pre-K through college English teachers offers journals, book publications, position statements, censorship resources, and networking opportunities. From lesson ideas to research, teachers can find resources tailored to their needs. NCTE is the publication home for this text, and they offer many others that complement and extend the thinking explored in this book.

Rethinking Schools

rethinkingschools.org
A nonprofit organization, Rethinking Schools publishes magazines, books, and other resources dedicated to advocacy, equity, and racial justice. Along with Teaching for Change, they host the Zinn Education Project.

Learning for Justice

www.learningforjustice.org
A K–12 resource site for teachers, Learning for Justice (formerly Teaching Tolerance) is focused on social justice and antibias work and offers classroom resources (arranged by grade level, topics, disciplines, and social justice domains), professional development, a magazine, and other publications.

Zinn Education Project

www.zinnedproject.org
Based on the approach of Howard Zinn's *A People's History of the United States*, this website promotes the classroom instruction of all people's history. It pushes back against traditional history textbooks in its more honest accounts of history. Teachers can download free lessons arranged by theme, time period, and grade level.

References

Allington, R. L. (2002). What I've learned about effective reading instruction from a decade of studying exemplary elementary classroom teachers. *Phi Delta Kappan*, *83*(10), 740–47.

Apple, M. W. (1971). The hidden curriculum and the nature of conflict. *Interchange*, *2*(4), 29–40, 71.

Apple, M. W. (1980). The other side of the hidden curriculum: Correspondence theories and the labor process. *Interchange*, *11*(3), 5–22.

Atwell, N. (1998). *In the middle: New understandings about writing, reading, and learning* (2nd ed.). Boynton/Cook.

Baker-Bell, A. (2020). Dismantling anti-black linguistic racism in English language arts classrooms: Toward an anti-racist black language pedagogy. *Theory Into Practice*, *59*(1), 8–21.

Baker-Bell, A., Butler, T., & Johnson, L. (2017). The pain and the wounds: A call for critical race English education in the wake of racial violence. *English Education*, *49*(2), 116–29.

Benedetti, A. (2011, June 15). Not just for teens: A 35 Going on 13 Special. *School Library Journal*. https://www.slj.com/story/archive/not-just-for-teens-a-35-going-on-13-special.

Bishop, R. S. (1990). Mirrors, windows, and sliding glass doors. *Perspectives: Choosing and Using Books for the Classroom*, *6*(3), ix–xi.

Bishop, R. S. (1992). Multicultural literature for children: Making informed choices. In V. Harris (Ed.), *Teaching multicultural literature in grades K–8* (pp. 37–53). Christopher-Gordon.

Bluemle, E. (2011, May 5). The stars so far: Yes or no? *Publishers Weekly*. http://blogs.publishersweekly.com/blogs/shelftalker/?p=4754.

Borsheim-Black, C., & Sarigianides, S. T. (2019). *Letting go of literary whiteness: Antiracist literature instruction for white students*. Teachers College Press.

Borsheim-Black, C., Macaluso, M., & Petrone, R. (2014). Critical literature pedagogy: Teaching canonical literature for critical literacy. *Journal of Adolescent & Adult Literacy*, *58*(2), 123–33.

Brabham, E. G., & Villaume, S. K. (2000). Continuing conversations about literature circles. *The Reading Teacher*, *54*(3), 278–80.

Briceño, E. (2016, December 1) *When performing gets in the way of improving* [Video]. TEDx Talk. YouTube. https://www.youtube.com/watch?v=KaiwGb0csas&t=144s.

Brown, A., & Mitchell, J. (with Kaywell, J., Bach, J., Buehler, J., Crowe, C., Richmond, K. J., Glenn, W., Scherff, L., & Bickmore, S. T.). (2014). The look of classic young adult literature. *The ALAN Review*, *41*(2), 6–14.

Buehler, J. (2016). *Teaching reading with YA literature: Complex texts, complex lives*. National Council of Teachers of English.

Butler, T., Penn, J. I., & Merry, J. (2020). "Pardon this disruption": Cultivating revolutionary civics through world humanities. In V. Kinloch, T. Burkard, & C. Penn (Eds.), *Race, justice, and activism in literacy instruction* (pp. 91–106). Teachers College Press.

Cammarota, J., & Fine, M. (Eds.). (2008). *Revolutionizing education: Youth participatory action research in motion*. Routledge.

Campano, G., Ghiso, M. P., & Welch, B. (2015). Ethical and professional norms in community-based research. *Harvard Educational Review*, *85*(1), 29–49.

Cart, M. (2001). From insider to outsider: The evolution of young adult literature. *Voices from the Middle*, *9*(2), 95–97.

Collins, B. (n.d.). *More About Poetry 180*. Library of Congress. https://www.loc.gov/programs/poetry-and-literature/poet-laureate/poet-laureate-projects/poetry-180/more-about-poetry-180/.

Crowe, C. (1998). Young adult literature: What is young adult literature? *English Journal*, *88*(1), 120–22.

Cunningham, A. E., & Stanovich, K. E. (1998). What reading does for the mind. *American Educator*, *22*(1–2), 8–15.

Daniels, H. (2002). *Literature circles: Voice and choice in book clubs and reading groups*. Stenhouse.

Delpit, L. (2006). *Other people's children: Cultural conflict in the classroom*. New Press.

Ehrenworth, M. (2020, June). *Foundations of a reading workshop* [Workshop Session]. Teachers College Reading Writing Project Summer Reading Institute, Columbia University.

Emdin, C. (2019, March 5). *Creating, debating, & #HipHopEd(ucating) at Google Fiber Space* [Conference presentation]. South by Southwest Education Conference & Festival, Austin, TX.

Fisher, D. (2009). The use of instructional time in the typical high school classroom. *The Educational Forum*, *73*(2), 168–76.

Fisher, D., & Frey, N. (2012). Motivating boys to read: Inquiry, modeling, and choice matter. *Journal of Adolescent & Adult Literacy*, *55*(7), 587–96.

Freire, P. (1985). *The politics of education: Culture, power, and liberation*. Bergin & Garvey.

Freire, P. (2000). *Pedagogy of the oppressed* (30th anniv. ed.). Continuum.

Freire, P., & Macedo, D. P. (1987). *Literacy: Reading the word and the world*. Routledge & Kegan Paul.

Gallagher, K. (2009). *Readicide: How schools are killing reading and what you can do about it*. Stenhouse.

Garcia, A., & Dutro, E. (2018). Electing to heal: Trauma, healing, and politics in classrooms. *English Education*, *50*(4), 375–83.

Garcia, A., & O'Donnell-Allen, C. (2015). *Pose, wobble, flow: A culturally proactive approach to literacy instruction*. Teachers College Press.

Gay, G. (2000). *Culturally responsive teaching: Theory, research, and practice*. Teachers College Press.

Ginsberg, R., & Glenn, W. J. (Eds.). (2019). *Engaging with multicultural YA literature in the secondary classroom: Critical approaches for critical educators*. Routledge.

Glenn, W. J., & Ginsberg, R. (2016). Resisting readers' identity (re)construction across English and young adult literature course contexts. *Research in the Teaching of English*, *51*(1), 84–105.

Glenn, W., Ginsberg, R., & King-Watkins, D. (2018). Resisting and persisting: Identity stability among adolescent readers labeled as struggling. *Journal of Adolescent Research*, *33*(3), 306–31.

Goldstein, D. (2015). *The teacher wars: A history of America's most embattled profession*. Anchor.

Grice, K. M., Murphy, C. E., & Shanahan, E. M. (2018). Taking out the trash: Complicating rural working-class narratives in young adult literature. *The ALAN Review*, *45*(3), 19–28.

Groenke, S. L., & Scherff, L. (2010). *Teaching YA lit through differentiated instruction*. National Council of Teachers of English.

Gross, M., & Latham, D. (2017). The peritextual literacy framework: Using the functions of peritext to support critical thinking. *Library & Information Science Research*, *39*(2), 116–23.

Guskey, T. R. (2018, February 4). Multiple grades: The first step to improving grading & reporting. *Education Week*.

Haddix, M., & Price-Dennis, D. (2013). Urban fiction and multicultural literature as transformative tools for preparing English teachers for diverse classrooms. *English Education*, *45*(3), 247–83.

Harlin, R., & Morgan, H. (2009). Review of research: Gender, racial and ethnic misrepresentation in children's books: A comparative look. *Childhood Education*, *85*(3), 187–90.

Herz, Sarah K., & Gallo, D. R. (2005). *From Hinton to Hamlet: Building bridges between young adult literature and the classics* (2nd ed.). Greenwood Press.

Ivey, G., & Broaddus, K. (2001). "Just plain reading": A survey of what makes students want to read in middle school classrooms. *Reading Research Quarterly*, *36*(4), 350–77.

Juliani, A. J. (2014). *Inquiry and innovation in the classroom: Using 20% time, genius hour, and PBL to drive student success*. Eye on Education.

Kasten, W. C., & Wilfong, L. G. (2005). Encouraging independent reading with ambience: The Book Bistro in middle and secondary school classes. *Journal of Adolescent & Adult Literacy*, *48*(8), 656–64.

Kelley, M. J., Wilson, N. S., & Koss, M. D. (2012). Using young adult literature to motivate and engage the disengaged. In J. A. Hayn & J. S. Kaplan (Eds.), *Teaching young adult literature today: Insights, considerations, and perspectives for the classroom teacher* (pp. 79–98). Rowman and Littlefield.

Krashen, S. (2006). Free reading. (Cover story). *School Library Journal*, *52*(9), 42–45.

Landt, S. M. (2006). Multicultural literature and

young adolescents: A kaleidoscope of opportunity. *Journal of Adolescent & Adult Literacy, 49*(8), 690–97.

Lee, C. C. & Schoonover, N. R. (2020). "My life's blueprint": Publishing critical youth narratives in community-based organizations. *English Teaching: Practice & Critique, 19*(1), 107–20.

Lesesne, T. S. (2010). *Reading ladders: Leading students from where they are to where we'd like them to be.* Heinemann.

Luke, C. (2000). New literacies in teacher education. *Journal of Adolescent and Adult Literacy, 43*(5), 424–35.

Marcus, L. S. (Ed.). (2021). *You can't say that! Writers for young people talk about censorship, free expression, and the stories they have to tell.* Candlewick Press.

McIntyre, A. (2000). Constructing meaning about violence, school, and community: Participatory action research with urban youth. *The Urban Review, 32*(2), 123–54.

Mirra, N., & Garcia, A. (2017). Civic participation reimagined: Youth interrogation and innovation in the multimodal public sphere. *Review of Research in Education, 41*(1), 136–58.

Moeller, R., Pattee, A., & Leeper, A. (2011). The young adult voice in research about young adults. *Journal of Research on Libraries and Young Adults, 2*(1). http://www.yalsa.ala.org/jrlya/2011/11/the-young-adult-voice-in-research-about-young-adults/

Moll, L. C., Amanti, C., Neff, D., & Gonzalez, N. (1992). Funds of knowledge for teaching: Using a qualitative approach to connect homes and classrooms. *Theory Into Practice, 31*(2), 132–41.

Morrell, E. (2008). *Critical literacy and urban youth: Pedagogies of access, dissent, and liberation.* Routledge.

Morrison, T. (1998, January 19). Interview with Charlie Rose. Public Broadcasting Service. Retrieved from https://charlierose.com/videos/17664.

Muhammad, G. (2020). *Cultivating genius: An equity framework for culturally and historically responsive literacy*. Scholastic.

National Council of Teachers of English. (2018). *Preparing teachers with knowledge of children's and young adult literature* [Position statement]. https://ncte.org/statement/chiladollitguideline/

Nilsen, A. P., Blasingame, J., Nilsen, D., & Donelson, K. L. (2012). *Literature for today's young adults.* (9th ed.). Pearson.

Ostenson, J., & Wadham, R. (2012). Young adult literature and the common core: A surprisingly good fit. *American Secondary Education, 41*(1), 4–13.

Oswald, R. A., & Smolen, L. A. (2010). Introduction to young adult literature. In L. A. Smolen & R. A. Oswald (Eds.), *Multicultural literature and response: Affirming diverse voices* (pp. 1-16). Libraries Unlimited.

Pandya, J. Z., & Ávila, J. (Eds.). (2014). *Moving critical literacies forward: A new look at praxis across contexts.* Routledge.

Paris, D., & Alim, H. S. (Eds.). (2017). *Culturally sustaining pedagogies: Teaching and learning for justice in a changing world.* Teachers College Press.

Petrone, R., Sarigianides, S. T., & Lewis, M. A. (2015). The youth lens: Analyzing adolescence/ts in literary texts. *Journal of Literacy Research, 46*(4), 506–33.

Roberts, K. (2018). *A novel approach: Whole-class novels, student-centered teaching, and choice*. Heinemann.

Rosenblatt, L. M. (1938/1995). *Literature as exploration* (5th ed.). Modern Language Association.

Skerrett, A., Warrington, A., & Williamson, T. (2018). Generative principles for professional learning for equity-oriented urban English teachers. *English Education, 50*(2), 116–46.

Smith, H. L., Flores, B. B., & González, D.A. (2016). Exploring the traditions of Latino children's literature: Beyond tokenism to transformation. In E. R. Clark, B. B. Flores, H. L. Smith, & D. A. González (Eds.), *Multicultural literature for Latino bilingual children: Their words, their worlds* (pp. 25–48). Rowman & Littlefield.

Spiering, J. (2017) Reviewing to exclude? Critical Discourse Analysis of YA LGBTQ book reviews for school librarians. *The ALAN Review, 44*(2), 43–53.

Stephens, J. (2007). Young adult: A book by any other name . . . : Defining the genre. *The ALAN Review, 35*(1), 34–42.

Tatum, A. W. (2009). *Reading for their life: (Re)building the textual lineages of African American adolescent males*. Heinemann.

Thein, A. H., & Kedley, K. E. (2015). Out of the closet and all grown up: Problematizing normative narratives of coming-out and coming-of-age in young adult literature. In D. Linville & D. L. Carlson (Eds.), *Beyond borders: Queer eros and ethos (ethics) in LGBTQ young adult literature* (pp. 3–20). Peter Lang.

Toliver, S. R. (2021). On windows, mirrors, and telescopes. *The Council Chronicle, 31*(1), 29–30.

Torres, F. L. (2019). Deconstructing the superhero: Interrogating the racialization of bodies using *All-New, All-Different Avengers, Vol. I*. In R. Ginsberg & W. Glenn (Eds.), *Engaging with multicultural YA literature in the secondary classroom: Critical approaches for critical educators* (pp. 162–70). Routledge.

Twenge, J. M., Martin, G. N., & Spitzberg, B. H. (2019). Trends in U.S. adolescents' media use, 1976–2016: The rise of digital media, the decline of TV, and the (near) demise of print. *Psychology of Popular Media Culture, 8*(4), 329–45.

Vasquez, V. M. (2017, March 29). Critical literacy. *Oxford Research Encyclopedia of Education*. https://oxfordre.com/education/search?siteToSearch=education&q=critical+literacy&searchBtn=Search&isQuickSearch=true

Vasquez, V. M., Janks, H., & Comber, B. (2019). Critical literacy as a way of being and doing. *Language Arts, 96*(5), 300–311.

Ward, B. A. (2010). Promoting multicultural literature and literacy: Awards, conferences, library initiatives, and outreach programs. In L. A. Smolen & R. A. Oswald (Eds.), *Multicultural literature and response: Affirming diverse voices* (pp. 403–22). Libraries Unlimited.

Wenger, E. (1999). *Communities of practice: Learning, meaning, and identity*. Cambridge University Press.

Wenger, E., McDermott, R., & Snyder, W. (2002). *Cultivating communities of practice: A guide to managing knowledge*. Harvard Business Publishing.

Wilhelm, J. (2015). Let them read trash! *English in Aotearoa. 85*, 16–22. https://scholarworks.boisestate.edu/cgi/viewcontent.cgi?article=1261&context=english_facpubs

Wilkinson, K., Andries, V., Howarth, D., Bonsall, J., Sabeti, S., & McGeown, S. (2020). Reading during adolescence: Why adolescents choose (or do not choose) books. *Journal of Adolescent & Adult Literacy, 64*(2), 157–66.

Wolfe, P. (2010). Preservice teachers planning for critical literacy teaching. *English Education, 42*(4), 368–90.

YA Titles Cited

Acevedo, E. (2018). *The poet X*. HarperTeen.

Adeyemi, T. (2018). *Children of blood and bone*. Henry Holt.

Adeyemi, T. (2019). *Children of virtue and vengeance*. Henry Holt.

Boulley, A. (2021). *Firekeeper's daughter*. Henry Holt.

Callender, K. (2020). *Felix ever after*. Balzer + Bray.

Chbosky. S. (1999). *The perks of being a wallflower*. MTV Books.

Chee, T. (2020). *We are not free*. Houghton Mifflin Harcourt.

Gansworth, E. (2013). *If I ever get out of here*. Arthur A. Levine.

Gansworth, E. (2020). *Apple: Skin to the core*. Levine Querido.

Grimes, N. (2019). *Ordinary hazards*. Wordsong.

Jackson, T. D. (2020). *Grown*. Katherine Tegen Books.

Jamieson, V., & Mohamed, O. (2020). *When stars are scattered*. Dial.

Mbalia, K. (2019). *Tristan Strong punches a hole in the sky*. Disney-Hyperion.

McKinney, L. L. (2018). *A blade so black*. Macmillan.

McKinney, L. L. (2019). *A crown so cursed*. Macmillan.

Nelson, J. (2015). *I'll give you the sun*. Dial.

Nguyen, T. L. (2020). *The magic fish*. Random House Graphic.

Pan, E. X. R. (2018). *The astonishing color of after*. Little, Brown.

Reynolds, J. (2017). *Long way down*. Atheneum.

Reynolds, J., & Kiely, B. (2015). *All American boys*. Atheneum.

Silvera, A. (2017). *They both die at the end.* Quill Tree.

Smith, C. L. (Ed.). (2021). *Ancestor approved: Intertribal stories for kids.* Heartdrum.

Smith, C. L. (2020). *Hearts unbroken.* Candlewick.

Stone, N. (2017). *Dear Martin.* Crown.

Tamaki, M., & Valero-O'Connell, R. (2019). *Laura Dean keeps breaking up with me.* First Second.

Thomas, A. (2017). *The hate u give.* Balzer + Bray.

Waid, M., Kubert, A., & Asrar, M. (2016). *All-new, all-different Avengers, Vol. 1: The magnificent seven.* Marvel.

Watson, R. (2017). *Piecing me together.* Bloomsbury.

Zoboi, I. (2017). *American street.* Balzer + Bray.

Index

Author

Ricki Ginsberg is an associate professor of English education at Colorado State University. She teaches courses in reading and writing pedagogies, teaching and research methods, and young adult literature. She was the 2020 president of the Assembly on Literature for Adolescents of the National Council of Teachers of English (ALAN), directs the Black, Indigenous, and Teachers of Color (BIToC) Collective at Colorado State University, is a faculty affiliate for the Race and Intersectional Studies for Educational Equity (RISE) Center, and is a former editor of *The ALAN Review*. Her first book, co-edited with Wendy J. Glenn, is *Engaging with Multicultural YA Literature in the Secondary Classroom: Critical Approaches for Critical Educators* (2019). Her work has been published in *The ALAN Review*, *American Indian Quarterly*, *English Journal*, *Journal of Adolescent Research*, *Journal of Education for Students Placed at Risk*, *Journal of Human Rights*, *Multicultural Perspectives*, *Reading Research Quarterly*, *Research in the Teaching of English*, *Teachers College Record*, and *Voices from the Middle*.

This book was typeset in Janson Text and BotonBQ by Barbara Frazier.

Typefaces used on the cover include American Typewriter, Frutiger, and Formata.

The book was printed on 60-lb. White Offset paper by Seaway Printing Company, Inc.